AF526676

ISLAMIZATION OF KNOWLEDGE

GENERAL PRINCIPLES AND WORK PLAN

Dr. Ismail al-Faruqi
Dr. Abdul Hamid Abu Sulayman

Qadeem Press

Qadeem Press

Qadeem Press Edition
Breathing Life into Forgotten Pages
www.qadeempress.com

Reprinted by Qadeem Press in 2025

Contents

Introduction

From the dawn of Qur'anic revelation to Prophet Muhammad (SAAS) to the "Call to Islam" (*da'wah*) and the establishment of the Ummah as a universal entity in Madinah, the Islamic community has faced immense challenges and conspiracies, manifested by direct military aggression and unrelenting psychological and economic warfare, covertly and deviously waged. Earlier, diverse opponents-pagan and heretic, Persian and Roman, among others-sought to trample the Ummah or to check its advance. Thanks to Divine Providence, however, the Ummah always emerged from these trials physically and spiritually stronger and more viable. In fact, in response to these assaults, the Ummah managed to strike at the root of many strongholds of disbelief (*kufr*) and to carry the message of Islam to far-flung regions of the earth, until it became the leading "nation" and the most balanced Ummah on Earth-an Ummah of the "Middle Way": "You are the best Ummah evolved for Mankind" (Qur'an, 3:110).

Because of repeated attacks, the initial enthusiasm and sense of commitment began to wane in later years; and the onslaught of enemies began to cause disintegration and weakness in the structure of the Ummah. Still, these enemies were unable to achieve an overall victory-one that could completely sweep away the Ummah's faith (*īmān*) and resolve.

After many attempts to achieve this desired objective foundered, these enemies set out to investigate and to search carefully for more devious methods. They concluded that the strength of the Ummah stemmed from its religion (*dīn*) and belief (*'aqidah*). Therefore, they launched an extensive campaign to weaken the Ummah's commitment and attachment to its *dīn*, Islam; to change its understanding and application of the *Shari'ah*; and to turn the great principles inherent in Islam from an active, motivating, and highly positive power into a rigid formalism that was incapable of inspiring or of directing the spirit and lives of Muslims.

This was the beginning of what may be designated as the intellectual incursion -a process that introduced (under the guise of logic, common sense, and pragmatism) certain philosophical and metaphysical concepts that led to much controversy and endless sophistry. The ensuing intellectual and religious consequences were disastrous for the Ummah. One result was the emergence of manifold esoteric (*batini*) sects, which further weakened the Ummah by impairing its unity and distracting its scholars from the original sources and unsullied fountainheads of Islam: the Qur'an, the Word of Allah (SWT), and the Sunnah of Prophet Muhammad (SAAS).

Another direct consequence of this intellectual incursion was the Muslim defeat at the hands of the Christian crusaders and the Mongols. Although the Ottomans temporarily saved the Ummah from its crisis, the effects of intellectual deviancy and the problems created by the partial application of the *Shari'ah* soon began to threaten the existence of the Ottoman State itself. During the age of the European Renaissance, the intellectual incursion began to assume new dimensions by becoming more systematic, all-embracing, and sophisticated.

Western imperialism, its religious functionaries, and orientalists' machinations together turned their campaign into a total and exhaustive onslaught. This campaign sought to crush any resistance to, infiltrating and transforming the Islamic mind and ethos. Islam, itself, had become the prime target to be penetrated. By isolating Islam from everyday life and twisting it into a dogmatic labyrinth, the cultural distortion and intellectual collapse of the Ummah was achieved.

At the beginning of the eleventh century A.H. / seventeenth century A.C., orientalists, colonialists, and missionaries laid the groundwork for this new intellectual offensive against Islam and the Ummah. They were aided and abetted, materially and morally, by numerous organizations and supporters, and succeeded eventually in ensnaring the hearts and minds of many Muslims, reshaping its thinking, and clouding their Islamic vision. When European industrialism and material progress reached their peak, Europe achieved prominence and power. At this same time, the Ummah was vastly depleted by lassitude, and its enemies decided to launch an all-out assault to deal the Ummah the final blow.

Following their victories in World War I, European armies occupied vast areas of the Muslim world. After this military occupation, they first implemented their well-researched policies for a complete intellectual take- over to ensure total estrangement of the Ummah from Islam. This estrangement would be passed on to all subsequent generations of Muslims.

Then, to create a wide gap between the Ummah and the main sources of the *Shari'ah* (the Qur'an and the *Sunnah*), the enemies introduced changes in all systems of education and only allowed the minimum amount of "Islamic" educational curricula. Moreover, their agents dominated and exploited the mass media, using intellectual and pedagogic pretexts to further facilitate the coveted transformation.

However, the struggle against colonialism and foreign indoctrination was never stamped out. The Ummah's spirit of struggle and resistance was sustained by the Qur'an, which was both a companion and a guide. The Qur'an provided daily reminders to Muslims of their place in history, their duty, and their predestined role of responsible world leadership: "Thus have we made of you an Ummah justly balanced, that you might be witnesses over the nations" (Qur'an, 2: 143) The Muslim spirit for struggle (*jihad*) and the underlying virtues of self-trust, self-esteem, and goodness were rekindled. This, in turn, led to the emergence of reformist and liberation movements in the Muslim world. Unfortunately, however, the approach and mentality of such movements betrayed a Western outlook and an alien methodology and frame of reference that doomed them to failure. Indeed, it is axiomatic that what is intellectually or ideologically good for Europe and the West, in general, is not necessarily good or suitable for the Ummah, whose existence and destiny are rooted in and dependent upon the Qur'an and the Sunnah.

Still, some movements tried to apply or advocate partial reform, wrongly assuming that they could succeed where others had failed in helping the Ummah regain its strength and greatness. The failure of these efforts and the resulting humiliation motivated other Muslim thinkers to devise other solutions. The Ummah had been entrusted with a mission, and the spiritual sustenance of its successive generations had always been found in the Qur'an and the Sunnah. Therefore, it was clear that any reform movement had to implement plans to help the Ummah derive its remedy from these sources, thereby regaining its identity and reestablishing a true Islamic life. It soon became apparent that the challenge that Muslim thinkers had to address was to offer a practical framework for understanding the Qur'an and the Sunnah. They needed to transfer the sources of knowledge from the realm of values, directives, and ideals into the realm of reality and practical application.

The crisis of the Ummah reached a peak when the West created an alien entity inside Muslim lands to act as a convenient springboard for its plans and ambitions. The creation of this entity through colonization by settlement, represents the most cruel and inhumane act of imperialism in the world. This was a further setback for the Ummah. Conscious of their identity, Muslims witnessed with chagrin the colonialists occupying their land, usurping their property and resources, degrading their character, defiling their sanctuaries, and ridiculing their religion. And, when the colonialists encountered feeble resistance, the sense of alarm in the hearts of Muslims reached unbearable limits. Shaken by such calamitous events, the Muslim mind was unable to distinguish between right and wrong or good and evil. Consequently, the Ummah was divided into more than fifty nation-states. This division occurred in such a way as to guarantee continuous friction among them. Many of these nation-states continue to fight each other rather than their enemies. This fighting encourages chaos and starvation to rampage over vast areas of the Muslim world.

Despite all this, and through the blessings of Allah (SWT), several groups within the Ummah have remained faithful to the truth and have adhered to their belief. Unwavering in their faith and regardless of prevailing suppression, corruption, and pessimism, they have tried to provide a map of the way to deliverance and salvation. One of these groups was made up of youth who had attained a clear understanding of the nature of the problem and its cure while still studying at various Western universities. Ironically, the frequently acrimonious reports they read about the malaise of the Ummah while they were in the West strengthened their resolve and determination to raise such questions as: Who are we? What do we want? and What should we do?

With the limited resources available to students, they began (with the enthusiasm of youth and the knowledge they had acquired) to convene small meetings to air their concern and to discuss views on the major problems facing the Ummah and the reasons behind its decline and disintegration. Their Ummah, they believed, had been endowed by Allah (SWT) with all the human, "ideological", and material resources that should guarantee power and dignity among the nations-yet, the malaise prevailed. After prolonged deliberations, they reached a conclusion, based upon both theorization and first-hand experience, that the basic cause of the malaise of the Ummah lay in its current thought processes which suffered from intellectual rigidity and stagnation. These young men believed that the minor crises the Ummah suffered were, in fact, mere products of the prevailing malaise and that intellectual deviation and stagnation had impaired the Ummah's thoughts, leading to loss of vision, confusion, disintegration, and weakness. Furthermore, they believed that previous sincere and genuine attempts at reform had failed because Muslim reformers had been unable to realize the role that deviation, distortion, and stagnation of thought and methodology had been playing in creating such aimlessness and impotence.

Cognizant of these facts, these young men established the Association of Muslim Social Scientists in 1382 A.H./1972 A.C. The Association addressed itself to the intellectual problems facing Islamic thought. They exchanged and disseminated information on all matters relating to Islamic thought, particularly among Muslim intellectuals. Though many of these young people were intellectually capable, they, nevertheless, refused to diagnose the malaise and its causes alone. They wanted to be absolutely sure that the diagnosis was correct and, therefore, contacted a number of Muslim activists (*du'at*) as well as contemporary Muslim scholars and reformers. The Association wanted to share with the others the ideas, concepts, and conclusions they had reached and to receive the benefit of the knowledge and experience of others. To this end, a decision was made to hold several meetings and seminars in order to exchange viewpoints.

In 1377 A.H. 1977 A.C., the Association sponsored a two-week international conference that was held in Europe for some of the most distinguished leaders of the Islamic movement. In addition to the Association which was, at the time, leading the students' Islamic movement in Europe and North America, thirty active leaders of Islamic movements and Muslim scholars in various fields of specialization from all over the Muslim world attended this meeting. The participants unanimously agreed that the contemporary crisis of the Ummah was intellectual-a crisis of thought-and that the remedy was to be sought within that framework. The seminar participants also concluded that the Muslim thought process and methodology needed to be given priority in the effort to achieve reform and that a specialized body needed to be established to conduct research into these areas. They emphasized that Muslim scholars needed to be involved. Those who attended were all capable and willing to address themselves to this issue and to help formulate a sound intellectual basis for the necessary purposeful, sincere, and methodical work.

The concerned young men lost no time as they began to gather resources for an independent scientific and intellectual organization to serve this purpose. Their efforts culminated in the establishment of the International Institute of Islamic Thought (IIIT). The Institute was officially incorporated in the United States of America at the beginning of the fourteenth Hijri century, and it immediately addressed itself to the issue of Islamic thought. Its first international conference was held in Islamabad, Pakistan (1402 A.H./1982 A.C.), in cooperation with the International Islamic University located there. The conference was attended by numerous Muslim scholars who presented various important papers and studies on the issue of Islamic thought and knowledge. They urged the participants to conduct research, to contribute to all scientific fields and social activities, to initiate educational and intellectual reform, to present alternative scientific concepts and solutions to problems, and to recast knowledge in the light of Islamic values, taking into account the realities of the contemporary world. The objectives of the conferences were to probe the causes of various aspects of the crisis of the Ummah and to determine priorities in the quest for a resurgence in working toward establishing the true mission of Islam. The papers, deliberations, and resolutions of the conference all confirmed the earlier convictions of those who had called for it. Practically all participants urged Muslim scholars to assume their responsibilities and to make all possible efforts to confront the intellectual aspects of the problem, which had previously never received the attention, or the priority required to stem the tide of cultural chaos and disintegration.

The plan formulated by the Institute to tackle the crisis of thought in the Muslim world has been based upon the conviction that the crisis involves two dimensions: the intellectual thought processes and the estrangement between the Ummah and its legacy, i.e. its alienation from its culture and civilization.

First, the intellectual incursion, change, and disruption that was introduced, especially in the social sciences and the humanities, was of such enormous proportions as to make the Muslims either overlook Islamic thought and legacy or, at best, to simply study it and treat it as an ancient phenomenon neither needed by nor relevant to contemporary life. Consequently, Muslim scholars and intellectuals sought to fulfil their needs in the Western social sciences, not realizing that the West had established these sciences in accordance with its own circumstances and goals and rooted in its ideological world vision. As a result, these sciences now tend to reflect the West's values, concepts, and beliefs, upon which all Western aspects of behaviour, activity, and social institutions are established. While these disciplines are acceptable and compatible with Western objectives, they tend to clash with Islamic values and guidelines. Much confusion has ensued, and the basis of the present conflict, contradiction, and loss of identity and direction can be traced back to contradiction and weakness in Islamic thoughts and aims. All this mandates as cornerstones in the attempt to cure the malaise and in the proposed change in the current systems of education in the Muslim world and the Islamization of the social sciences, as well as in regaining our intellectual identity.

Second, the plan draws attention to the current estrangement between the Ummah and its legacy-a rift that has turned Islam's great achievements into merely historical ones-mere fossils of a bygone age, recalled, if at all, to muster nostalgic feelings or an ineffectual sense of pride. The legacy of Islam, to many, no longer presents the basis for dynamic creativity.

The Institute, therefore, believes that the Ummah must be united under the aegis of its legacy, that the legacy should be viewed as a viable and dynamic force. The Institute believes that many aspects of this legacy can be used to the Ummah's advantage through methodical and effective planning geared to making the presentation and understanding of the educational and intellectual heritage of Islam easy and accessible. It realizes that this can be accomplished by systematically arranging and classifying the legacy and by establishing the specific relevance of Islam to the modern disciplines and social sciences. Indeed, this legacy, as it stands today, is often obscure and yields its treasures only to a few capable and patient scholars. As a result, the Institute, *Inshaa Allah,* intends to prepare and publish its Agenda for classifying the Islamic Legacy. In addition to this, there will be model studies that are intended to provide the modern Muslim disciplinarians with ready access to the Legacy in their areas of specialization.

Following the Conference in Islamabad on the Islamization of knowledge (1402 A.H./1982 A.C.), the Institute decided to publish a detailed plan to serve as a guide to Muslim intellectuals and students in the field of Islamization of knowledge. The result was the publication of *Islamization of Knowledge: General Principles and Workplan,* based upon papers and speeches delivered at various conferences by Dr. Ismail Rājī al Fārūqī and Dr. Abdul Hamid Abū Sulayman. The late Dr. al Fārūqī took the initiative in editing the first edition, while Dr. Abū Sulayman re-edited, updated, and introduced the plan in a subsequent Arabic edition.

In this second English edition, edited by Dr. Abū Sulayman, the first four parts of the original English edition remain basically unchanged, however, some important modifications and additional concepts and ideas have been presented. The new edition offers greater understanding of the intellectual issues facing the Ummah and the Muslim scholars-not in the field of education but foremost in thought and methodology.

These concepts will also put forth a new frame of reference and approach to life for the Ummah and the Muslim mind. This will, *in shaa Allah*, lessen or eliminate the prevailing apathy (*tawākul*) and revive the Muslim attitude of seriousness and efficiency, action and perfection toward life (*itqān*). It is this attitude which constitutes an integral part of the Muslim concepts of *Khilafah* (vicegerency), *Işlāh* (reform), and *I'mar* (civilization) in this world.

This edition also offers a more dynamic and precise work plan for Islamization of Knowledge by IIIT. It reflects the interaction between increased knowledge and the increased involvement of the scholars in the process of thinking and writing in the field-the process of "learning through doing". It emphasizes the Islamic vision and an original approach of methodology of knowledge, incorporating the three Islamic sources of knowledge: revelation (*wahy*), reason (*aql*), and the universe (*al kawn*). This edition affirms that Islamization of knowledge is a continuing process and that its major goals are achieved through the accumulation and development of ideas in the various fields of knowledge.

Moreover, the new edition seeks to further clarify (see part 7) the concept of Islamization of knowledge, its relevance and relationship to "westernization," "modernization," and the dynamics of actual life and events. These clarifications and emphasis are worth the notice of the readers, especially in acquiring a firm grasp of the idea, mission, and priorities involved in the concept and task of Islamization.

Rabi' al Akhir 1409 AH
November 1988 AC

Chapter I: The problem

A. The Malaise of the Ummah

The Ummah of Islam stands at present at the lowest rung of the ladder of nations. In this century, no other nation has been subjected to comparable defeats or humiliation. Muslims were defeated, massacred, double-crossed, colonized, and exploited, proselytized, forced, or bribed into conversion to other faiths. They were secularized, Westernized, and de-Islamized by internal and external agents of their enemies. This occurred in practically every country and corner of the vast Muslim world. Even though they were victims of injustice and aggression on every count, Muslims were vilified and denigrated in representations of them in all nations. They enjoy the worst possible 'image' in the contemporary world. In today's global mass media, the 'Muslim' is stereotyped as aggressive, destructive, lawless, terroristic, uncivilized, fanatic, 'fundamentalist, backward, and anachronistic. Muslims are the objects of hatred and contempt on the part of non-Muslims, whether developed or underdeveloped, capitalist or Marxist, Eastern or Western, civilized or otherwise. The Muslim world itself is known only for its inner strife and division, its turbulence and self-contradictions, its wars and threats to world peace, its excessive wealth and excessive poverty, its famines, and epidemics. In the minds of people everywhere, the Muslim world is the "sick man" of the world; and the whole world is led to think that, at the root of all these evils, stands the religion of Islam.

The inexorable facts that the Ummah numbers over a billion people; that its territories are among the vastest and the richest; and that its potential in human, material, and geopolitical resources are the greatest, make the defeat, the humiliation, and the misrepresentation of Muslims intolerable. What aggravates this even further is the knowledge that the Ummah's faith- Islam-is, in fact, an integral, beneficial, world-affirming, and realistic religion in which practical solutions for contemporary problems of humanity can be sought and found.

B. Major Effects of the Malaise

1. Political Character

The Ummah is divided against itself. The colonial powers have successfully fragmented the Ummah into some fifty or more nation-states and set them one against another. The boundaries of the Muslim states have been so defined as to create perpetual friction for every state with its neighbours. Political machination by the enemy continually exploits those areas of friction and creates feelings of alienation and hostility.

Internally, every Muslim nation-state is, in turn, divided against itself because its population is heterogeneous, and one group is assigned hegemony over the other groups by the colonial masters. No nation-state was given the time, peace, or resources necessary to integrate its own citizenry into a single entity; and no two states were allowed to unite so as to constitute a greater whole. Indeed, the few attempts in that direction were doomed to failure. To make things worse, the enemy either has imported aliens into the Muslim world in order to guarantee perpetual strife and to initiate reasons. for interference in the internal affairs of these states or has converted groups of natives of those states to a Western Christianity that necessarily implies their estrangement from their Muslim compatriots or has infused into non- Muslim natives a notion of their ethnic identity that sets them in conflict with the Muslims. Finally, the enemy has created hostile "foreign" states within the body of the Ummah to divert Muslim energy away from reconstruction, to drain its resources in futile wars, or to serve as bases for colonialism and foreign political interests. Every Muslim government spends the greater part of its resources and energy on securing its own power within and its sovereignty without-and yet without avail.

Throughout the Muslim world, except in a few regions where the enemy has found rulers ready to cooperate, colonial administration has destroyed all political institutions in the land. When the time came for colonial administrations to withdraw, they entrusted power to the native elites who had already been systematically Westernized. Then, in most former Muslim colonies, power went to the military who were destined to grab it at the first opportunity. In the majority of cases today, Muslim countries are ruled by the military because they are devoid of political institutions that are capable of operating the government, of mobilizing the masses for resistance, of leading them into constructive political action, or, simply, of acting in harmony with one another.

2. Economic Character

The Ummah is non-developed and backward. The overwhelming majority of its members are illiterate. Their production of goods and services is far below their needs, which are then satisfied by importing finished goods from colonial and postcolonial powers. Even in the strategic necessities of life- the staple foods, clothing, energy, and hardware-no Muslim state is fully self-sufficient. Just about every Muslim state would be exposed to famine if the colonial powers wished for any reason to stop their unfair trade with them. Everywhere, colonial interest has been creating consumer markets and demands for colonialists' products, while the needs of Muslims for productive hardware goes unheeded. In their competition with local Muslim productivity, the colonialists seek (and often succeed) in forcing it out of the market. When the colonialists help to develop some industry, it turns out to be one that is dependent upon the colonialists' raw materials or finished components, which they alone supply, thus subjecting the industry to function at the colonialists' mercy, thereby subserving their goals. In most cases, the new Muslim industries are not designed to meet the basic needs but, rather, those tangential needs created by colonialist all-pervasive advertisement. Muslim agricultural self-sufficiency is their first enemy, since, at this stage and for a long time to come, that is the prerequisite of Muslim resistance to any colonialist scheme. Muslim farmers are uprooted from their villages by false promises of better living in the cities, through the lure of temporary jobs in speculative building-construction and consumer-goods industries, and through exploitation by landlords and tax collectors. The farmers migrate to the cities to live in shanty towns, dependent upon imported staple foods, and become prey to any demagogue who capitalizes upon their adverse circumstances.

The oil bonanza with which Allah (SWT) endowed some Muslim countries has not proven to be the blessing (*nimah*) it was supposed to be. Scanty population distribution, in addition to intellectual and cultural decline and political instability, contributed to this. In most instances, the new wealth produced cosmetic development and, therefore, failed to play its natural role in developing the agricultural and industrial potential of the Ummah.

Rather, it is still being channelled for "easy and secure" investment in the financial markets of the non-Muslim world, thus helping to develop foreign economics.

3. Cultural Character

The centuries of decline have caused illiteracy, ignorance, and superstition to spread among Muslims. These evils have caused the average Muslim to withdraw into the bliss of blind faith, to lean toward literalism and dogmatism, or to surrender himself to superstitions and to various charlatans. All these aberrations have bred in the Muslim no small measure of vulnerability. When the modern world imposed itself upon the average Muslim, his military, political, and economic weakness caused him to panic. He sought half-measures of reform that, he thought, would speedily recapture for him his lost ground. Unwittingly, he took to Westernization, lured by the successful example of the West, and prompted by his Eastern or Westernized advisers. In areas under colonial administration, Westernization was ordered and promoted by every possible means at the rulers' disposal.

Well-meaning or otherwise, Westernized Muslim leaders did not grasp the fact that their programs would sooner or later undermine the very foundations of the faith and culture of their subjects. The connection between the manifestations of Western productivity and power and the Western views on God and man; on life, nature, the world; and on time and history was too subtle for Muslim leaders to grasp or, in their hurry, to consider. A secular system of education was built that taught Western values and methods. Soon, graduates who were ignorant of the Islamic legacy began to pour into society. The new graduates became suspicious of the majority of the guardians of the legacy, the *ulama'*, who were dogmatists, legalists, and literalists, who failed to distinguish between those juristic verdicts (*ahkām*) of the Qur'an and the Sunnah that could not be discarded or dismissed, and those matters that are open to creative exercise of judgment (*ijtihad*). The graduates' suspicion of the guardians of the legacy increased and a gap began to develop within the ranks of the Ummah, dividing it into Westernizing secularizers and opponents of secularization. The colonialist powers saw to it that the former became the decision makers in society.

The colonialists attacked everything Islamic either directly or by their native puppets. The perfection of the Qur'anic text, the Message of the Prophet (SAAS), the veracity of the Sunnah, the comprehensiveness of the Shariah, and the glories of Muslim achievements in culture and civilization were severely denigrated; none of them were spared. The purpose was to inject doubt into the Muslim's confidence in himself, in his Ummah, and in his faith and ancestors. The object was to undermine his Islamic consciousness and to subvert his Islamic personality. Because he lacked the spiritual stamina. necessary for resistance, he was susceptible to corruption. The colonialists and their stooges filled the Muslim's daily life with media products that promoted Western culture. Newspapers, books, and magazines; radio and television; cinema and theatre; records and tapes; and street posters and neon signs bombarded him daily with such effects. Muslim governments took pride in the new boulevards they opened in their capitals, which were dotted with Western-style high-rise office or apartment buildings; but they were not shamed by the squalor and degradation of the rest of their towns and villages. Westernized elites frequented public halls to watch a movie or to listen to an opera, a concert, or a drama; and their sons and daughters read about them in books in public or missionary schools and colleges, without realizing their incongruity with everything else they thought or did. Those who completed their self-Westernization stood out more oddly against their Muslim environment and background. The integrity of Islamic culture and the unity of the Islamic style of life were shattered in their own persons, in their thought and actions, in their homes and families. Western social institutions and customs were introduced into their lives in excess and with impertinence. Instead of raising themselves from their debasement to the heights of virtue and societal efficacy envisaged for them by Islam, Muslin men and women began to hanker after the manifestations of Western decadence: gradual nudity and immorality of dress and make-up (*tabarruj*), economic independence aimed at individualistic license, egotistic pursuit of pleasure, and avoidance of duties imposed by family relationships.

In the cities, Islamic architecture died, and Islamic town planning became non-existent. The overgrown urban centres repeated every mistake and shortcoming of the European city that underwent the industrial revolution two centuries ago, as if utterly incapable of learning from the experience of others. Muslim homes, furniture, art, and decoration became a hodgepodge of all styles, betraying confused notions of Muslim identity.

Despite all claims that he has Westernized himself, the Muslim has, in fact, barbarized himself. His life has become a conglomeration of styles, discontinuous with his selfhood. He has made of himself something neither Islamic nor Western a cultural freak of modern times.

C. The Core of the Crisis: The Malaise of Thought and Methodology

There can be no doubt that the intellectual and methodological decline of the Ummah is the core of its malaise. The educational system is the breeding ground of the disease. Schools and colleges generate and perpetuate that self- estrangement from Islam, from its legacy, and from its style. The educational system is the laboratory where Muslim youth are kneaded and cut, where their consciousness is moulded into a caricature of the West. Here, the Muslim's link with his past is severed; his natural curiosity to learn the legacy of his fathers is stymied. Here, his willingness to touch base with his heritage and to spring toward creative representation of Islam is blunted by the doubts and the deviation the educational system has injected into every recess of his consciousness.

1. The Present State of Education in the Muslim World

Despite the tremendous expansion that has taken place in education so far, the state of Muslim education is at its worst. As far as Islamization is concerned, never before have both the traditional and the secularist schools, colleges, and universities been more daring in advocating their un-Islamic themes, and never before have they had the captive ear of the overwhelming majority of Muslim youth as they do today. Since its inception under colonialist administrations, the secularist educational system has assumed tremendous proportions, elbowing out the Islamic system from the field. Islamic education, for the most part, remains a private affair that has limited access to public funds. Where public funds are made available, demands of secularization are imposed in the name of modernism and progress. This usually consists of bifurcating the curriculum into contrasting-nay, opposing-components, one Islamic and one "modern". What took place in some well-known Islamic universities is a classic example.

The colonialists devised a well-thought out and well-planned strategy. The Islamic component of the curriculum in certain universities remains unchanged, partly because of conservatism and vested interests, and partly because it is in the secularist plan to keep it out of touch with reality and modernity. In this way, their graduates will present no competition to those of the secular institutions.

National independence gave the secularist educational system its greatest boost by adopting it as its own, pouring public funds into it, and secularizing it even further in the name of racist nationalism and regional "patriotism", The forces of Westernization and secularization, and resultant de-Islamization of teachers and students, continue to gather momentum in colleges and universities; and nothing has been done to arrest that degeneration. In fact, the situation is worse than it was under colonialism. Under colonialism, a spirit of resistance, of searching for liberation and an Islamic solution, animated nearly everyone. Today, students are cynical, lethargic, and mistrust all leaders. This is largely due to repeated false promises and disappointments, and to the sad example of a morally bankrupt leadership. No Muslim government, university administration, or private organization is doing anything about the sinking morale of college youth or about their continuing de-Islamization through "education". The colossal building programs in the affluent Muslim countries and the consequent growth of student bodies, faculty members, and expansion of facilities all serve the secularist cause. Hardly any of the funds are devoted to "modernizing" in a genuine sense, i.e., to improving the quality of education and the Islamic orientation of students and faculty. Everywhere, the race is on at maddening speed toward completing the Western educational model.

2. Lack of Clear Vision

Despite all claims to the contrary, the net result achieved is not a Western model, but rather a caricature of it. Like the Islamic model, the Western educational model depends ultimately upon a specific vision, though different from that of Islam, and is animated by a will to realize that vision. Buildings and offices, libraries and laboratories, and classrooms and auditoriums teeming with students and faculty are all material paraphernalia of little worth without the requisite vision. It is the nature of such vision that it cannot be copied, only its incidentals can. That is why, in nearly two centuries of Westernized, secularized education, the Muslims have produced neither a school, college, university, nor a generation of scholars that matches the West in creativity or excellence. The insoluble problem of low standards in the Muslim World institutions is a necessary consequence of this lack of vision. There is no genuine search for knowledge without spirit, and the Western spirit is precisely what cannot and should not be copied. It is generated by its own vision of life and reality, in short, by its faith.

Education in the Muslim world lacks this vision. Its leadership does not have the vision of the Western man by necessity; and it does not have the vision of Islam by its own choice, i.e., by deliberate ignorance, laziness, and lack of concern. Educational leadership in the Muslim world has existed without culture and without cause. Nationalism has inspired the Western universities in the last 200 years because Romanticism has replaced the defunct

God of Christianity with "la nation" as the genuine "ultimate reality". For the Muslim, no reality is ultimate but Allah (SWT). Therefore, ultimate loyalty to the nation-state, is both impossible and blasphemous to him. Whatever type of link a Muslim has with his legacy and past, it is not possible for him to be a "nationalist" in the same sense as the European who has substituted his Christianity with his 'nationalism'.

Look at the highest model of the Muslim university teacher- the professor with a doctorate from a Western university, especially in the social sciences and humanities. He was trained in the West and graduated with a fair or less than fair average. In most cases, he was not Islamically motivated beforehand, i.e., he had not embarked upon his expedition to seek knowledge. for the sake of Allah (SWT), but rather for a materialistic, egoistic, or at best, nationalistic goal. Therefore, he did not obtain all the knowledge available to him in the West, nor did he surpass his Western teachers at their own game; nor did he, like his ancestors (who learned and Islamized the sciences of ancient Greece, Persia, and India), digest what he learned or seek to rehabilitate it within the Islamic vision of knowledge and truth. Rather, he was satisfied to pass, to obtain the degree, to return home, and to achieve a position of affluence and eminence. The books he read as a student constitute the ultimate reaches of his knowledge; for now, he has neither time, energy, nor motivation to push beyond the frontiers of his basic training. His living and working conditions add to his distraction from such a distant ideal. Naturally, his students must emerge even less motivated and less competent. For them, the Western ideal has receded even further. Gradually, the standards sink; and Western education in the Muslim world becomes a caricature of its Western prototype.

The subjects and methodologies presently taught in the Muslim world are copies of the Western ones but are devoid of the vision that animated them in the West. Devoid of that vision, they have become instruments of mediocrity. Unconsciously, these dispirited materials and methodologies continue to exert a sinister de-Islamizing influence upon students by posing as alternatives to the Islamic disciplines as well as agents of "progress" and "modernization". They make the graduate of the Muslim university a typical "freshman"-thinking that he knows a great deal but knowing very little indeed.

The very possibility of excellence in the Western disciplines is, thus, removed from the Muslim student. For that possibility requires that the student perceive the totality of knowledge in his chosen field as well as become motivated by a driving idea to appropriate and to transcend this totality. The former depends upon the latter, since, in order to acquire knowledge of the totality, one must be driven by a consuming idea that only commitment to a cause generates. Without a cause, the Muslim is not driven to master the totality of knowledge in the discipline; and, without that mastery, no transcendence of the discipline's state-of-the-art is possible. For the Muslim, the only cause that can really be a cause is Islam. Lacking it, the Muslim. teachers who studied in the West never reached the totality of knowledge. As teachers in universities, they could never impart this requisite of excellence to their students. Content to copy and to translate the less-than-totality of knowledge that they had acquired, they and their students are, at best, doomed to a mediocre performance.

That teachers in Muslin universities do not possess the vision of Islam and, therefore, are not driven by its cause is certainly the greatest calamity of Muslim education. Throughout the Muslim world, students enter the university equipped, as far as the Islamic vision is concerned, with the little knowledge of Islam they acquired at home or in elementary or secondary school. Obviously, this constitutes no "vision" and no "cause". Ideologically, therefore, the freshman student enters as a blank sheet. He may come with sentiments but surely not with ideas. These sentiments, if any, are shipwrecked when confronted with the "ideas", "facts", and the objective judgments of "science" presented to him in the disciplines. Obviously, he has no defences nor vision with which to counter this ideational level. If he does not graduate a confirmed atheist, secularist, or communist, his view of Islam has receded to a realm of personal, subjective, and sentimental attachment to family and people. He does not envision Islam as vibrant, replete with the best and most relevant ideas concerning any problem. On the ideational level, the student in a Muslim university confronts alien ideologies presented to him in textbook or classroom with as miserable a defence as a soldier who, armed only with lance and sword, confronts an enemy armed with tank and machine gun. Nowhere in the Muslim world is the Islamic vision taught to all students as the Western tradition is taught to high school students in the West, i.e., with consistency, universality, utmost seriousness, and commitment on the part of all. In no Muslim university is such a vision part of the "basic" or "core" studies program that is compulsory to all students.

Chapter II: The Task

The greatest task confronting the Ummah in the fifteenth Hijri century is to solve the problem of education. There can be no hope of a genuine revival of the Ummah unless the educational system is revamped, and its faults are corrected. Indeed, the system needs to be formed anew. The present dualism in Muslim education, its bifurcation into an Islamic and a secular system, must be removed and abolished once and for all. The two systems must be united and integrated, and the emergent system must be infused with the spirit of Islam and must function as an integral part of its ideological program. It should not be allowed to remain an imitation of the West; nor should it be left to find its own way; nor should it be tolerated that it serves merely the economic and pragmatic needs of the student for professional training, personal advancement, or material gain. The educational system must be endowed with a mission, and that mission must be none other than that of imparting Islamic vision and cultivating the will to realize it on the largest scale.

Such a task, looked upon narrowly, is indeed difficult to perform and may be costly in comparison with what is currently being allocated for education. But the Ummah spends a far lesser percentage of its gross national product and of its annual budget on education than do most other nations in the world today. Those nations know how to develop and to safeguard their educational systems; and they, therefore, realize the benefits obtained by spending money wisely on these systems. Even in those affluent Muslim countries where the budgets for education are significant, the major expenditure is on buildings and administration rather than on research and proper educative activities. The Ummah must spend far more on education than it presently does in order to attract the best minds and to help them achieve what is expected of them, as well as to maintain the dignity Allah (SWT) has bestowed upon them as "men of knowledge" or "seekers" of it.

A. Integrating the Two Educational Systems

To establish a unified educational system in which Islam is the motivating and guiding power, the Islamic educational system, which consists of elementary and secondary schools (*ma'ahid ilmiyah or diniyah*) as well as colleges (*kulliyāt*) and universities (*jāmi'āt*), must be united with the secular system of public schools and universities. The union should bring to the new unified system the advantages of both, namely, the financial resources of the state and the commitment to the vision of Islam. Unifying the two systems. should create the opportunity to eliminate their major shortcomings, namely, the inadequacy of archaic textbooks, the inexperience of many teachers in the traditional system, and the mimicry of the secular West in methods and ideals in the public system.

The advantages may be gathered by the new system if the respective governments agree to appropriate for it the necessary funds without exercising stifling control. Steps must be taken to make the new educational system financially secure, if not wholly independent, by promoting endowments (*waqf*-continuous self-supporting charity) the income of which would fund the total system or at least part of it. Such endowments are precisely the *awqaf* that the Shariah recognized and protected for the welfare of the Ummah. In the past, it was the *waqf* of each school (*madrasah*) that made it autonomous and thus enabled its teachers and students to seek knowledge for the sake of Allah (SWT) alone, which is the necessary condition for any successful search for the truth. And it was the waqf institution that gave the madrasah the first legal or corporate personality in history. It was the waqf-based *madrasah* that constituted the model emulated by the first universities of the West when they were founded eight centuries ago.

Because of the explosion of knowledge, as well as the student population, education may be too expensive today to be funded by endowments alone. A yearly portion of public funds may well be necessary. The state, however, must develop the wisdom necessary to negotiate the amount of the subsidy with the educators and trust them to make the best possible use of it. If state universities in the West can do this, it is unjustifiably presumptuous to claim that Muslims acting under Qur'anic injunctions are incapable of the same. There can be neither a good nor promising future in an Ummah that does not respect its learned sons and daughters, nor exerts itself to transmit to them the cultural and spiritual legacy of their ancestors, nor enables its youth to add to and enrich their tradition. It is a sign of tyranny when the state does not trust its educators to do their job without policing the educational establishments. And it is a sure sign of decadence when political rulers tell educators what to teach and how to run the academic function.

B. Instilling the Islamic Vision

The union of the two education systems is expected to do more than bring means to the Islamic system and autonomy to the secular. It is expected to bring Islamic knowledge to the secular system and modern knowledge to the Islamic system. It is criminally negligent to entrust Muslim youths at the elementary and secondary education levels to missionaries or non- Muslim educators; this must be stopped. Every Muslim youth is entitled to receive full instruction in the religion, ethics, law, history, and culture of Islam. The Ummah or any section of it, as well as its leaders, are legally responsible and, in the justice of Allah (SWT), criminally indictable if they fail to give instruction in Islam, including its conceptions and objectives, to every Muslim child.

The same is, at the least, as crucial in the case of adult education. The child's spirit is protected by his parents or guardian, who will see to it that he commits no act odious to Islam nor violates any provision of the *Shari'ah.* The adult, on the other hand, is free. He is the target of anti-Islamic propaganda in and outside the university. In the college classroom and through assigned reading projects, he is constantly presented with alien ideologies in the name of science and modernism. Anti-Islamic ideas and options for conduct are claimed to constitute scientific truth, to be based upon objective fact. Islam was presented to the Muslim student, in his tender years, with the voice of parental authority. His mind was not mature enough to understand or to appreciate "objective" claims. His attachment to the Islamic position, therefore, was born out of sentiment, not out of reasoned conviction. Evidently, his commitment to Islam cannot withstand the onslaught of "scientific", "objective", or "modern" truth. This is why, in the absence of any counter-presentation of Islamic understanding-a presentation made with the same force of objectivity, the same scientific orientation, and the same appeal of modernity- the Muslim college student succumbs to the secular claim and converts to it. So begins the process of de-Islamization in Muslim universities.

After four years of such alienating influence within the university and an equal, if not superior, influence stemming from the mass media, his peers, and society, the Islamic consciousness of the Muslim youth is ravaged. No wonder that he becomes a cultural freak, a cynic who is at home neither in Islam nor in the West, ready to be swayed by anyone who caters to his whims of the moment.

1. Mandatory Study of Islamic Civilization

An important aspect of the possible antidote to this de-Islamization on the university level is a mandatory four-year study of Islamic civilization. Every student in the university must undertake this course of study regardless of his or her area of specialization. The fact that they are citizens, members of the Ummah, imposes upon them the need to acquire a viable amount of knowledge of the Ummah's legacy, an adequate command of the Ummah's spirit, and familiarity with its civilization. It is not possible to be civil without such knowledge. Even if students belong to a non-Muslim minority, it should not absolve them from fulfilling this basic requirement. Since they or their parents have opted to become citizens of the Islamic state, they must acquire the necessary familiarity with the civilization in which they are living and with the spirit and hope that move this civilization and its compatriots.

No person may be left without such acculturation, which is basic for "socialization" or integration into Muslim society. Only such a study can immunize students against invading ideologies by enabling them to meet argument with argument and objective evidence with objective evidence. Only such a study can prepare them for genuine participation in the cultural life and progress of the Ummah, for only through it will they learn the essence of Islamic civilization, the logic of Islam, and the direction in which the Ummah is heading or is hoping to head. Only through it will they learn how to distinguish their Ummah and, hence, themselves from the others and to feel proud of this distinction, anxious to maintain it, and to pull the others to identify with it.

The study of civilization is the only way to foster in the person a clear sense of identity. No one may be said to be self-conscious who is ignorant of ancestors; nor the spirit that animated them; nor their achievements in the arts, sciences, politics and economy, social organization, or aesthetic experience. Neither is one self-conscious who is unmoved by the travails, tragedies, glories, and victories of his ancestors or who is uninspired by their hopes. The consciousness of self-identity is not achieved except when such knowledge of one's background is contrasted with knowledge of other peoples, groups, and civilizations. To know oneself is to know how one is different from others, not only in material needs or utilitarian realities but, also, in the view of the world, in moral judgment, and in spiritual hope. This is all the domain of Islam, of the culture and civilization that Islam built and sustained through the generations. It is achievable only through the study of Islam and its civilization and through the comparative study of other religions and civilizations.

Today, to be "modern" is to be civilizationally conscious, i.e., to be conscious of the nature of one's civilizational heritage, of the essence that produced its various manifestations, of its distinction from other streams of civilizational history and of its pull and direction for the future. Without such knowledge, one cannot be the master of one's own fate; and, certainly, one cannot survive in this world. Unlike the past, the civilizational forces contending in this century can reach and overtake anyone without invasion or military occupation of his land. They can subvert his mind, convert him to their world view, neutralize and contain him as a puppet whether he is aware of it or not. Certainly, these forces are contending with one another to dominate the world. And it is the decision of Muslims today whether Islam will be the victor tomorrow, whether Muslims will be makers of history or merely its objects. Indeed, the civilizational battle now in progress in the world scene will not leave anyone unscathed. Every human is bound to be transformed by one contender or another, unless he himself prevails over the contending civilization and is, therefore, a transformer of others.

It is unbecoming of Muslims to argue that Islamic civilization will remain alive as long as it is taught in the departments or institutes of Islamic studies in the universities and colleges of the *Shariah.* Indeed, it is indicative of their decadence that Muslims have instituted "departments of Islamic studies" in their universities. These are always copies of departments of Oriental studies in Western universities, where the study of Islam is the specialization of the few whom society needs for administering its relations with the Muslim world. On the other hand, although the need for specialists in the Shariah to end the disputes among Muslims will always require the high training the colleges of the *Shari'ah* provide, knowledge of the *Shari'ah* must be made available. to all members of the Ummah. Everybody must have a viable mastery of the sciences of the Shariah since it constitutes the norm (*minhaj*) or method of Islamic existence.

The knowledge of Islam and of its civilization is not meant for the few. The vision of Islam is not meant for, nor needed by, the specialist alone. It is for all humans and is designed to elevate all those who possess it to a higher level of existence. Islam abhors the division of humans into cleric and lay; it insists that all men are to know, teach and observe the truth. Indeed, the Prophet (SAAS) said: "It is obligatory for each Muslim, male or female, to seek knowledge." The vision of Islam is needed to defend the whole people against alien ideologies invading their consciousness. Unless everybody is immunized against the disease, the Ummah will become the victim. Moreover, Islam is the comprehensive religion the vision of which is relevant to every human activity and to every endeavour whether physical, social, economic, political, cultural, or spiritual. It is not an other-worldly religion like Christianity and Buddhism, content to deal with "divine" affairs and to leave the rest to Ceasar. Islam is relevant to everything said or done in any shop or factory, office or home, theatre or field, university classroom or laboratory. An Islamic vision cultivated in only one department or faculty would be a truncated vision of Islam. It must be the guiding, determining, first principle of every discipline of every pursuit and of every human action.

What is needed, therefore, is an educational system in which the curriculum of every department is based upon Islamic values, principles, and objectives. Furthermore, a four-year course on the principles of Islam as the essence of Islamic thought and civilization must be introduced as part of the "basic" or "core" program for all students, regardless of their field of specialization or profession. This course will be designed to give the Muslim student the values and first principles of Islam as the essence of Islamic civilization, as well as the historical achievements of Islamic civilization as manifestations of the first principles of Islam. The course will include discussions of how Islamic civilization compares and contrasts with other civilizations in essence and manifestations. It also will give the Muslim student knowledge of how Islamic civilization is the only viable option in dealing with the fundamental problems of Muslims and non-Muslims in the contemporary world.

2. The Islamization of Modern Knowledge

It would be a great step forward if Muslim universities and colleges were to institute requisite courses in Islamic civilization as part of their basic studies program for all students. This will provide the students with deeper faith in their own religion and legacy and give them the confidence in themselves to enable them to face and surmount their present difficulties as well as to forge ahead toward the goal assigned to them by Allah (SWT). But this is not enough.

In order to forge ahead toward this Islamic goal and, thus, to make the word of Allah (SWT) supreme everywhere, knowledge of the world is absolutely indispensable. This knowledge is the goal of the disciplines. Before Muslims went into decline and slumber, they had developed the disciplines and had established and clarified the relevance of Islam and its comprehensive world view and values to each discipline. They successfully integrated the disciplines into the main corpus of Islamic knowledge. They contributed greatly to all fields, and they utilized the new knowledge efficiently to their advantage. Today, non-Muslims are the undisputed masters of all the disciplines. In the universities of the Muslim world, non-Muslim books, achievements, world- view, problems and ideals are currently being taught to Muslim youths. Today, Muslim youth are being Westernized by Muslim teachers in Muslim universities.

This situation must be changed immediately. There can be no doubt that Muslim academicians must master all the modern disciplines in order to understand them completely and to achieve an absolute command of all that they have to offer. This is the first prerequisite. Then, they must integrate the new knowledge into the corpus of the Islamic legacy by eliminating, amending, reinterpreting, and adapting its components as the worldview of Islam and its values dictate. The exact relevance of Islam to the philosophy and the method and objectives of each discipline needs to be determined. A new way in which the reformed discipline can serve the ideals of Islam must be determined and a new trail must be blazed. Finally, by their example as pioneers, Muslim academicians must teach successive generations of Muslims and non-Muslims how to follow in their footsteps, to push the frontiers of human knowledge ever further, to discover new layers of the patterns of Allah (SWT) in creation, and to establish new paths for realizing His will and commandments in history.

The task of Islamizing knowledge (in concrete terms, to Islamize the disciplines or, better, to produce university-level textbooks recasting some twenty disciplines in accordance with Islamic visions) is among the most difficult to realize. As far as we can tell, no Muslim has yet contemplated the contradiction of Western knowledge with the vision of Islam. It is our present generation that first discovered this conflict as we live it in our own intellectual lives. But the spiritual torture this conflict has inflicted upon us caused us to wake up in panic, fully aware of the rape of the Islamic soul taking place before our very eyes in the Muslim universities. That is why we are alerting the Muslim world to the evil and seeking for the first time in history to elaborate a plan to arrest it, to combat its effects, and to relaunch Islamic education on its proper track, leading to its predestined goal, with the grace of Allah (SWT).

It is most regrettable that the Muslim world is still devoid of a centre where thinking and planning on such high level takes place.

What is needed is a university that acts as headquarters for Islamic thought, where the disciplines undergo Islamization, and the process is tested in the classrooms and seminar rooms of the undergraduate and graduate programs of study. Until the International Institute of Islamic Thought (IIIT) was established, not one educational institution in the Muslim world had planned to tackle the issue of the Islamization of knowledge, to produce Islamic textbooks for college use in the disciplines or to provide the tools of research necessary. for writing those textbooks. And, yet, everywhere in the Muslim world, one hears of the need to Islamize education, its men, and its institutions and to prepare alternate curricula and textbooks. On the official level, where the power to make decisions lies, one finds little more than lip service, which addresses men's emotions without having any essence or relation to practical execution and application in the classrooms.

The Islamization of knowledge is the noblest of all tasks, the most important cause animating and driving its adherents. The least argument in its favour is that Muslims have no other choice but to lend their souls to determination by a cause if they want to stop being the objects of history and to become its makers. And, yet Islam is not another "ism" on a par with these movements nor does it present its claim as its own, as a dogma personally; experienced and subjectively appropriated; that can only be adopted or dropped arbitrarily. The assertion of Islam is rational, necessary, and critical-one that addresses the mind and the intellect. It has universal validity, an ought-assertion, and title to the acknowledgment and acquiescence of mankind. As a rational claim, it can be met only with counter argument, which the Islamic adherent should welcome and to which he should respond with Islamic evidence and authentication. No part of the Islamic assertion, no relevance of

Islam to any discipline, may be accepted without convincing evidence. This is possible only when the Islamic vision has made its claim and has established it upon the basis of the most exacting scholarship, when it has substantiated it for the most fastidious conscience and can be rejected or resisted only out of irrationality or malice.

This is then the great task facing Muslim intellectuals and leaders: to recast the whole legacy of human knowledge from the viewpoint of Islam. The vision of Islam would not be a vision indeed unless it represented a special content; namely, life, reality, and the world. The content is the object. of study of the various disciplines. To recast knowledge in the mould of Islam relates to the Islamic vision. It is necessary to Islamize knowledge, i.e., to redefine and re-order the data, to rethink the reasoning and relate the data. to reevaluate the conclusions, to re-project the goals and to do so in such a way as to make the disciplines enrich the vision and serve the cause of Islam. To this end, the methodological categories of Islam-namely: the unity of truth, the unity of knowledge, the unity of humanity, the unity of life and purposeful character of creation, and the subservience of creation to Man and of Man to Allah (SWT)-must replace the Western categories and determine the perception and ordering of reality. So, too, should the values of Islam replace the Western values and direct the learning activity in every field. The Islamic values concern:

(a) the usefulness of knowledge for man's felicity.

(b) the blossoming of his faculties.

(c) the remoulding of creation so as to crystalize the Divine patterns and values of Islam.

(d) the building of culture and civilization.

(e) the building of human milestones in knowledge and wisdom, heroism and virtue, piety, and righteousness.

Chapter III: Traditional methodology

1. Shortcomings

Through the Tartar invasion from the East and the Crusader invasions from the West, non-Muslims devastated the Ummah. These invasions caused the Ummah to disintegrate into a number of nation-states. This disintegration caused, in turn, disagreement among Muslims. Fearing that weak and self-centred rulers would manipulate religious matters and issues, Muslim ulama became over-conservative and protective. They sought to preserve their most precious possession-Islam-as well as their own identity by proscribing all innovation and by advocating strict adherence to the letter of the Shariah.

The major source of creativity in the *fiqh* of the *Shari'ah* is ijtihad, i.e., creative self-exertion to derive laws from the legitimate sources. When an *'alim* can find no precedent within the Qur'an and the Sunnah for solving a given issue, he must recourse to ijtihad. However, and in their fear, the 'ulama abandoned ijtihad and declared that the *Shari'ah* was perfect in its present state as developed by the works of the ancestors. They, therefore, declared that any departure from it is an innovation, and that every innovation is undesirable and condemnable. Consequently, the *Shari'ah*-as elaborated by the schools of thought (*madhāhih*) was to become frozen. This only, the 'ulama believed, could safeguard the survival of Islam.

These feelings, attitudes, and mentality behind the conservative measures prevailed from the eighth to the twelfth centuries. The survival of Islam, and indeed Muslim victories and expansion in Europe during this period, did nothing to undo these restrictive measures. In the absence of ijtihad by which Islam had earlier thrived, some Muslims tried to overcome the difficulties they faced in a changing world by adopting *tasawwuf* (Sufism) and its turuq or "ways" as a substitute for a more balanced practice of Islam.

By stifling individual creative thought, the scholars doomed the Shariah, and thus Islam, to stagnation and decline. The *fiqh* remained a closed system until modern times, even when modern science and technology provided the West with the power to confront and defeat the Muslims.

In modern times, the West undid the Ottoman conquests in Europe. They occupied, colonized, and fragmented the whole of the Muslim world except Turkey proper, from which the Western powers were driven by force, and Yemen and central and west Arabia, which provided little incentive for colonization at that time. The Western powers exploited Muslim weakness to the utmost and contributed to a great extent to the present malaise of the Muslim world described in the first pages of this book. In response to the defeats, tragedies, and crises that the West had imposed upon the Muslim world in the last two centuries, Muslim leaders in Turkey, Egypt, and India have tried to Westernize the Ummah in the hope of making it politically, economically, and militarily viable. Wherever such an attempt was made, it was a failure. Indeed, it continues to be a failure today, and one that is more striking the more consistently it is applied, as in Turkey and Egypt. In Turkey, it prepared the way for Mustafa Kamal Ataturk to abolish all Islamic institutions and to reject every traditional Islamic principle affecting public life. Western institutions were substituted for the whole Islamic system and its legislation. Today, after two generations (nearly sixty years) of Westernization, Turkey is just as weak and poor in all respects as other Muslim countries.

Westernization did somewhat succeed in de-Islamizing the educated class of society and, additionally, caused weakness and retrogression, but it did nothing else. In Egypt, where Westernization was less consistently pursued, a Western system was implemented, and the traditional Islamic system was permitted to function alongside it. The two systems competed with each other; and, despite the tremendous advantages the Western system enjoyed (such as public funds, government support, and favours), both failed to achieve excellence. Their competition, however, succeeded only in weakening each other as well as the Ummah.

2. *Fiqh* and Fuqaha' (Islamic Law and Jurists)

The term "*fiqh*" means, in the terminology of the *fuqahā*, knowledge of the practical juristic judgements (*ahkam*) of the *Shari'ah*, which is attained by intellection of their detailed evidence. Its derivative, "*faqih*", refers to the person endowed with such knowledge. However, *fiqh*, according to common contemporary usage, means possession of knowledge of all judgments of the Shariah. Such knowledge presupposes command of the Arabic language, of the judgmental (*hukmi*) passages of the Qur'an and Sunnah, as well as the mental ability to determine their purpose. Evidently, it is a technical meaning, highly restricted when compared with that of the Qur'anic usage of the root (*fa- qa- ha*), reported in numerous verses, which point to intellect and understanding, to grasping the essence and explanation of Islam as a whole. The great jurists of Islam-al Shafi'i, Abū Hanifah, Malik, and Ahmad ibn Hanbal-all understood the comprehensive term "*uşül al fiqh*" to mean the evidence of the judgment of the Shariah and the first principles of Islamic understanding of life and reality. Part of that is, of course, understanding the general principles of the judgment of Islamic *fiqh.*

Moreover, the early fuqaha' of the Ummah, namely, the companions (ṣahābah), their successors (*tăbiin*), and the great founders of the *fiqh* schools (RAA), were pre-eminently knowledgeable in all matters affecting the lives. of Muslims. These *fuqaha'* of the classical early period maintained an encyclopaedic knowledge; they were masters of practically all the disciplines- from literature and law to astronomy and medicine. They were themselves professional men and women who knew Islam as law and additionally, as ideal and theory, as a system of thought and life, lived and practiced by millions. The highest and most important Islamic qualification ever, namely "*al dhawq al shar'i,*" or the intuitive *shar'i* knowledge of the purposes of the law, was well within their grasp, in addition to a natural sound disposition.

If the early *fuqahā*, due to their superb training and competence, were models of creative handling of the lives of the Muslims they counselled, however the training and knowledge of today's *faqih* does not adequately equip the person to assume the role of the early *fuqaha'* who had carried out very successfully their duties and responsibilities in guiding the lives of Muslims. A great number of graduates from the present day Shari'ah and Islamic colleges are not sufficiently trained by the curricula of these institutions. Ibn Taymiyah and his student, Ibn al Qayyim, were among the first to call for a reopening of *ijtihad.* They were later followed by a number of *'ulama* and *du'ät*, until the twelfth Hijri century when Muhammad Ibn Abd al Wahhab began to actively pursue the same direction through his movement. His call was adopted by Muhammad Abduh and his teacher, Jamaluddin al Afghani, as well as by other *'ulama* and *du'är.*

Although awakened Muslims everywhere approved the call to reopen the gates of ijtihad, the movement failed for two reasons:

First, the traditional qualifications required of the *mujtahidun* remained the same as before and, thus, restricted the practice of ijtihad to the graduates of the traditional institutes, i.e., to those who saw no need for it. The graduates of the traditional institutes had received an education that convinced them that the methodology was adequate, and that the problem of the Muslim world was merely one of human reluctance to realize the values of Islam.

Second, the understanding of the mujtahid, by definition the *faqih*. The *faqih* is a person whose training in *fiqh* and whose knowledge of Shari'ah has enabled him to translate all contemporary social problems into legal terms and to make pronouncements upon them under the categories of the law. This approach contained or subsumed the problems of modernity under the categories of Islamic *fiqh* and contained its verdict, which was pronounced according to one or more of the traditional schools of jurisprudence. The role of Islam in society and life became confined only to legal terms. This restricted ijtihad still further by concentrating all its efforts upon *ifta'* or "the pronouncement of *fatāwā* (juristic verdicts given by an *'ālim* on any specific daily action or matter pertinent to Islamic law). This bypassed the necessary alternatives needed to realize the Islamic vision and to establish a social order based upon Islamic concepts and goals. Thc traditional training of a faqih or a mujtahid undoubtedly pulled him away from such insight and kept him captivate in a restricted circle in which he sought to correlate and to harmonize current social practices and the juristic verdicts relating to them according to one or more traditional schools of *fiqh*. Such limited practice and conception called for inevitable efforts to reform the traditional methodology and to introduce a new Islamic methodology. A great number of traditional 'ulama were incapable of conceiving either the manifestations or the dimensions of this new methodology in the process of reviewing as well as reopening our very understanding of the *usül*, or sources of Islamic knowledge.

3. The Opposition of Revelation (*Wahy*) to Reason (*'Aql*)

Probably the most far-reaching development in the intellectual history of the Ummah is the dichotomy between revelation and reason. It was the advent of Greek logic and its influence upon some Muslims, who were all too anxious to utilize the methods it provided to convince non-Muslims of the truths of Islam, that made them indulge in futile theological issues that, eventually, led to a perceived separation of *Wahy* from *Aql*. Hellenized Christians and Jews lived for centuries under the aegis of this dichotomy, and many brought it into the Ummah with them when they converted to Islam. Al-Farabi gave this dichotomy its classical statement upheld by the philosophers against the theologians (*mutakallimün*). The dichotomy was accepted by some later *mutakallimün* who were content to elaborate on the faith defensively. Such logic continued to dominate the field of intellectual discussion in the age of decline, especially under the influence of sufism, which was influenced by Gnosticism. Sufism advocated a purely intuitive and often esoteric methodology, and, hence, found no fault with estrangement between reason and revelation.

Unlike those religions that sought to overwhelm man's understanding and to overpower his conscience so as to surrender to the irrational, or even the absurd, the call of Islam was rational and critical. Invariably, it invited men to use their intelligence, to apply their critical faculties to all claims, to consider the alternatives, to always be cogent and coherent, to say nothing but the truth of which one is absolutely certain, to always seek correspondence with reality and to shun conjecture, guessing, and supposition. Practically every page of the Qur'an contains such exhortations, injunctions, and commands. Without reason, the truths of revelation cannot be appreciated; nor can they be recognized for what they are; namely, Divine, and acknowledged as such. The claims of revelation would then become indistinguishable from other claims, including the absurd. When acceptance of revelation is not based upon reason, it is subjective, arbitrary, and whimsical. No religious theses based upon personal whims could claim the acquiescence of mankind or of any significant part of it for a long time. When some Muslims placed exaggerated emphasis upon the intuitive at the cost of reason, they unwittingly opened the gates to corruption of the Islamic faith and mind. By not distinguishing things rationally as being fake and absurd, superstition and old wives' tales certainly masqueraded as truth and penetrated the faith. Just as surely, the over emphasis of "reason" at the cost of intuitive faith corrupted the "life of reason" by reducing it to materialism utilitarianism mechanism, and meaninglessness.

4. The Separation of Thought from Action

In the early period of Islamic history, the leader was the thinker, and the thinker was the leader. The vision of Islam was dominant, and the zeal to realize it in history determined all the conduct and the goals of the Ummah. It was the preoccupation of the whole community of Islam. Every conscientious Muslim sought to probe reality for new creative Islamic patterns to enrich the existence of Islamic life. The faqih could, at the same time, be a leader of prayer (*imam*), mujtahid; reciter of the Qur'an (*qāri'*); scholar of the traditions (*muhaddith*); teacher, theologian (*mutakallim*), as well as political, military leader, farmer, businessperson or professional. If the *faqih* felt weak in any of these roles, everybody around him was eager to step in and make up the deficiency. Everybody gave freely of all that they had to the cause, and everybody felt more solidly strong because of the strength of others. Muslims were so closely associated with one another that the weakness of any one of them was quickly overcome by the solidarity and total experience of all. Since Islamic thought was, by nature, oriented toward reality, it was compelled by it to keep its gaze focused upon the real commonweal of living men and women. If that period witnessed little speculative or metaphysical thought, the reason is not that they were incapable of it but that the priority for most Muslim thinkers lay in enabling the masses of people to lead healthy, rational, virtuous and prosperous lives.

On the other hand, the actual life of the people, being the object of continuing thought on the part of their leadership, had the immediate benefit of the thinkers' creative ideas. Adequate thought was applied to the problems of the Ummah, and the solutions fitted the requisites of the situations. The Ummah prospered in every facet of thought and life; for its welfare and interest were constantly in view of the best minds, and the solutions projected by them were implemented and protected because the same minds commanded the executive power or were closely associated with those who did.

Later, this unity between thought and action was broken. The moment they were separated from one another, each began to deteriorate. Political leadership and the men of power moved from one crisis to another without the benefit of thought, without consulting the learned and obtaining their wisdom. The results alienated the wise subjects and *'ulama* and isolated them from reality and the important vital concerns of the people.

On the other hand, the leadership was isolated from the sources of Islamic thought. Eventually, this gap grew wider. Put on the defensive, the political leaders perpetrated still more and greater mistakes.

The thinkers, estranged and removed from active engagement in the Ummah's affairs, retreated to the ideal as grounds for their condemnation of political authority. Some began to indulge in affirming the normative over and against the actual. Those whose condemnation carried political consequence were subjected to persecution by the leadership in power. Others whose condemnation did not, were encouraged to soar still higher away from reality. Other thinkers began to compromise the normative in their association with the political leadership. Increased tension led to polarity, and this brought about the ruin of both thought and action. Whereas action became tyrannical and succession to power became violent, thought, having abandoned empirical reality and the real commonweal of the people, contented itself with commentaries on older works or took to mystical flight in mystic Sufi speculation. Soon, the whole Ummah became impervious to its own political leadership. The long succession of tyrants, corrupt leaders, throne usurpers, and puppet caliphs manipulated by powerful men, demoralized the Ummah and repulsed it from the political scene. Consequently, the gnostic Sufi brotherhoods received people with open arms. They provided them with spiritual self-discipline and cultivation of mystical experience and, thus, allowed them to be resigned to this in the face of their loss on the scene of history. In their hands, mystical experience provided an escape from the tyranny that none could confront or bear.

Soon, while the sultans reigned without challenge, some of the greatest mental energies of the Ummah were channelled toward spiritual, personal, and subjective values contemplated by *tasawwuf*. The equivalence and convertibility of the spiritual and the worldly, characteristic of the early period, disappeared. In its place came the pursuit of the spiritual at the cost of the worldly, of the other world at the cost of this world. Losing its anchor in the actual experiences of the Ummah, Muslim thought became conservative and literal in law, speculative in Qur'anic exegesis and world view, world- denying in ethics and politics and esoteric in the sciences of nature. Great thinkers, jurists, and highly respected people all looked down upon political authority and action as something beneath them, in itself contemptible. At first, resistance to the world-indeed, outright rejection of and then complete disregard for it-became the first conditions of virtue. The Ummah seemed to have lost the balance between the personal and the public values so subliminally exemplified by the Prophet (SAAS) in his life.

5. Mundane and Religious Dualism

Al Şirat Al Mustaqim, or "the straightforward path," which was the hope of all the early Muslims, was a single, unitary path stemming from the vision of Islam and integrating all of man's tendencies and activities into one integral surge toward Islamic self-realization in history. In the period of decay and because of the estrangement between thought and action, the path split in two: the way of the world and the way of virtue. This bifurcation of Islamic life into two paths in constant opposition to each other (the one condemnable and involving the material world with all its values and the other praiseworthy and involving all the religious and ethical values) corrupted and destroyed the role of the two paths, and both were eventually transformed. The former became empty spirituality, similar to the spirituality of Christian and Buddhist monkhood. A spirituality that does not concern itself with the empirical welfare of the masses and does not seek to actualize justice all over a world that is rampant with chaos, corruption, and manipulation, must be subjective, bent upon the religious interest of the adherent alone. Such spirituality is egotistic and individualistic, even when it calls for altruistic acts, for its prime concern is the state of consciousness of the practitioner, not of the Ummah. For the egotistic spiritualist, the non- practitioning masses and their welfare are mere tools and instruments of self-trial, self-purification, and self- ennoblement. No wonder that this spirituality fell to the lure of gnosis and to the mystical experience and became the prey of superstition and miracle- mongering. It never initially occurred to the virtuous leaders and great minds who laid the philosophical and ideological foundations for what later became Sufi turuq that their followings would become brotherhoods and aberrate. in such a manner and develop an ethic and a hope that ran counter to Islam. However, most brotherhoods did succumb to this temptation.

The path of the world, on the other hand, developed its own immoral system, absolved, as it were, from the moral requirements that the representatives of the religion of Islam declared to be the specialized pursuit of another class of Muslims. Without moral values as internal to and constitutive of it, this system was bound to deteriorate and become the prize for anyone who could contend for it successfully. Thus, government and political leadership or office became instruments for self-glorification and brute exercise of power or for extorting moral and material benefits from the people. When, in the modern period, the foreign colonial enemy attacked, invaded, and occupied Muslim lands, the masses barely resisted. They had already become convinced that the battle was not theirs. Finally, when the colonial administrations set up an alien educational system and began to favour a style of life, thought, and activity alien to that of the masses, they regarded it as a new trend, condemnable and contemptible but not worthy of strong and immediate action by the whole Ummah against it.

Chapter IV:
First principles of Islamic methodology

The fundamental prerequisite for effective overall reform of the Ummah is the Islamization of knowledge. Emphasis needs to be placed upon eliminating the gulf between thought and action, between idealism and realism, and between the ideological leadership on one side and the socio-political leadership on the other. The Islamization of knowledge also is indispensable for removing dualism in the educational system. In the interest of Islamizing knowledge, a number of principles that constitute the essence of Islam must be unfailingly observed. These principles constitute the framework of Islamic thought and methodology; they are the lighthouse that guides Islamic mentality, psychological build-up, and personality in academic and everyday life.

In the past, much distortion of the Islamic image resulted from the confusion between the precepts of logic and the tenets of the Muslim's personality, mentality, and methodology of acquiring knowledge and living his life. This confusion hampered the driving force of the Islamic spirit and kept it from realizing its sacred mission of toil, reform, creativity, and construction on earth.

The appearance on the Islamic scene of intruding nations with noted heritage of civilization and learning created new cultural and religious challenges for the Ummah. Due to cloudiness of Islamic vision, the new challenges were met by a sophistry that was alien to the Islamic faith. This alien sophistry was responsible for the ensuing philosophizing about the nature of Divinity, the attributes of Allah (SWT), destiny, and the causal concept of existence. Such philosophizing was alien to Islamic belief, which is characterized by its simple presentation of the facts of life as given by revelation in a way feasible for the human mind to comprehend, provided that that mind is protected from unfounded philosophic speculations.

The following sections present the fundamental principles that Muslims should thoroughly grasp and observe as the framework of Islamic thought, methodology, and way of life.

A. The Unity of Allah (SWT)

Allah (SWT) is the One and Only, begets not, nor is He begotten, and nothing is like unto Him. He has created the earth and the universe and willed that man would be entrusted by vicegerency on the earth that he might construct and diffuse good on it and face reckoning in the hereafter. These are the eternal facts brought forth to man by revelation. All other principles and concepts that lack the ability to comprehend fully Divine justice and aims and the purpose in creating man, short of sizing man's limited mental powers and dependence upon Divine Providence, are excluded.

Such is the framework of Islamic belief that our good predecessors knew. It stands in striking contrast to the distorted vision and methodology of later generations. Those generations went astray when it came to believing in the facts of existence and related metaphysical concepts. The outcome was that they deviated from Islamic thought to the extent of rocking the very foundations of the understanding of the role of revelation in guiding man. Logicians and philosophers even had a negative concept of the relationship between revelation and reason. This fact emphasizes the importance of purifying Islamic knowledge from the pitfalls of sophistry and alien metaphysical concepts that corrupted the Islamic methodology of thought and education.

Islamization of knowledge should, by definition, recast modern disciplines within the framework of Islamic principles and ends, thereby bringing back to normalcy the Islamic vision, methodology, education, and personality. This is the way to reassert the dynamism of the individual and collective Islamic existence and vitality.

The unity of Allah (SWT) is the first principle of Islam and of everything Islamic. It is the principle that Allah (SWT) is indeed Allah (SWT), that no other being is Allah (SWT), that He is Absolutely One, and that everything else is separate and different from Him as Creator.

To turn to Him and to seek Him is to seek goodness, justice, and truth, which is the noblest of goals symbolizing the highest plane of existence.

He is the Creator by Whose command everything that is has come to be and by which every event that happens has come to happen. He is the source of all goodness and beauty. His Will is the law of nature, as well as the law of morality. All creatures, above all humans, owe Him His worship and praise. Allah (SWT) created humans in the best of forms, endowed them with faculties with which to recognize Him and acknowledge His works, and gave them the capacity to transform creation so as to fulfil therein His ethical and aesthetic patterns. Mankind has been given free will and, through free exercise of that will, can choose either to learn truth and goodness that will lead to achieving the welfare of the Ummah or to suffer by opting for falsehood, evil, and corruption.

To think and live in consciousness of Divine unity, who is Justice itself, is to do so in a world of order, justice, and progress. Since everything in the world is there by the act of Allah (SWT) and is sustained by His providence, nothing is futile or devoid of meaning. Everything in the Creator of Allah (SWT) is according to a precise measure that Allah (SWT) has ordained for it. To be part of such a world is to recognize one's practically infinite complexity of relationships with all creatures, above all to acknowledge one's creatureliness, to attribute one's indebtedness to Allah (SWT), and to give Him His due of love and obedience. To be a Muslim is to have Allah (SWT) constantly present in one's consciousness. Since He is the Creator and the Judge, to be Islamic means to do all and everything as He has directed and for His sake. All good and all happiness, as all life and all energy, are His gifts. In Islamic life, these are acknowledged and used as such; while, in Islamic thought, He is the first and ultimate cause and end of everything. As such, His being and activity are the first constitutive and regulative principles of all knowledge. Whether the object of knowledge is the microcosm of the atom or the macrocosm of the stars, the depths of the self, the conduct of society, or the march of history, Islamic knowledge regards the object of knowledge as materially caused by the antecedent constituents of the situation whence that object preceded. The actual discharge of causality that brought about the object out of an infinity of other possibilities to which those same constituents might have led, is the initiative of the Divine Being, issuing from the Divine Command.

As for us humans, to accept Islam entails accountability in this life with faith, belief, and adherence to His will. It entails struggle and action rather than verbal professing, sophistry, and conjecture; and it entails rejecting negligence, indifference, and indolence.

Likewise, Islamic knowledge regards every object of knowledge as fulfilling an end that is willed by Allah (SWT) or that serves another end which is so willed, so that the causal hierarchy of the universe is at once a hierarchy of ends, at the top of which stands the Divine Will, willing the end of every individual being, of every series of ends, and of the hierarchy as a whole. Islamic knowledge recognizes that there is neither being, nor truth, nor value outside the parameters and complexes in which Allah (SWT), Who is the Truth, is cause and end, both immediate and ultimate; that whatever is conceived of, known, or evaluated outside the divinely ordained nexus is non-existent, false, value-less, or merely misrepresented as standing outside that nexus.

B. Unity of Creation

1. Cosmic Order

From the unity of Allah (SWT), the unity of His creation follows with logical necessity. As He has said in the Qur'an: "If there were in heaven and earth other gods than Allah, both heaven and earth would have fallen into chaos." (Qur'an, 21:22). If there were more than one ultimate reality, ultimate reality would not be ultimate. Moreover, the universe would then have to follow different orders; and, if it did, it would not be the ordered universe we know. Nor would it be possible for us humans to know a universe in which more than one order prevailed. Cosmic order, it must be remembered, is that under which we discern objects as substances, qualities, relations, and events. It is the consistency or unity of cosmic order that enables us to recognize the permanence of substances as things and the repetition of events as causal relations. Without cosmic order, neither things nor causes and consequences would be the same.

Creation is an integral whole precisely because it is the work of the Creator, whose order and design have infused every part of it. Cosmic order consists of the laws of nature. These operate throughout the universe and permeate every part and aspect of it. The material, the spatial, the biological, the psychic, the social, and the aesthetic realities all obey and fulfil these laws. All laws of nature are the *Sunan* (patterns) of Allah (SWT) in His creation. Allah (SWT) is more than the source of these laws. Having once designed nature according to them and established their working in nature, He continues to operate and control them. He is not a retired Allah (SWT) but is eternally living and active. Therefore, every being in the cosmos, and every event that takes place, does so by His command. At any stage of its existence, every being has built within itself the dynamic power to change. This dynamic power comes from Allah (SWT) and is sustained by Him. Furthermore, this power is not necessarily bound to produce the result with which it is associated. It is by the command of Allah (SWT) that a particular effect is caused, not by the causes usually associated with it. Allah (SWT) may activate a cause to bring about its effect immediately; but He may and does operate a cause by means of other causes, so that what seems to us to be an inexorable chain of causes is just as much a divine cause as a single cause. For our part, as humans, we trust Allah (SWT) and his cosmic order: that, given a cause, its effect will follow. As al Ghazālī and Hume had discovered, despite their ideological differences, there is no necessity to any causal connection. Indeed, what we call causality is mere "following upon" and repetition, leading us to believe that a cause is usually followed by its effect. Such faith has nothing to stand upon except the benevolence of the Divine Being. For Allah (SWT) seeks not to cheat nor to misguide. He is a benevolent Creator Who ordered things in the universe to make it liveable and comprehensible to us; to make it possible for us to exercise our moral options and to prove our ethical worth in our deeds.

2. Creation: A Kingdom of Ends

Allah (SWT) created everything and did so with precise measure (Qur'an, 25:2). This measure assigns to everything its nature, its relations to other beings, and the course of its existence. Equally, the divine measure subjects everything both to the system of causes described above and, also, to a system of ends. Everything has a purpose which its being serves. This purpose is never final but is always subject to other purposes constituting a final distillation that ends only in Allah (SWT). For only He is the ultimate End, the final Purpose, unto Whom everything returns. His Will makes everything called good actually be good.

Everything that is, therefore, is at once related in a cause-effect relationship to everything else, as well as in a finalistic, or means-to-end, relationship. For both the metaphysical and the axiological relationships terminate with Allah (SWT). The network of each is infinite, ending with Allah (SWT). Certainly, both are open for human inspection, for human knowledge and appreciation. Being finite, however, humans can only know a portion of the relationships-led, as it were, by a pocket flashlight in a dark jungle. But it is their prerogative and duty to press ever forward in exploring and discovering these relationships. To discover and establish these relationships is to establish, for knowledge and appreciation, the immutable patterns of Allah (SWT).

All things in creation serve a purpose and all purposes are interrelated, as a means and an end to one another. This makes the world one telic system, vibrant and alive, full of meaning. The birds in the sky, the stars in the firmament, the fishes in the depths of oceans, the plants and the elements - all constitute integral parts of the system. No part of it is inert or evil, since every being has a function and a role in the life of the whole. Together, they make an organic body whose members and organs are interrelated. Humans are only now beginning to make limited discoveries through science, of how the parts of nature are interrelated.

Muslims know all too well that creation is organic, that every part of it serves some end or another, even if that end is not known to them. This knowledge is a consequence of their faith. Confronted with the wolf devouring the lamb, the bird eating the butterfly, or the human corpse feeding the worms in the earth, they assume all beings to be good, fulfilling in their natural activity a divine purpose and serving a system of purposes that culminates in the Divine Will. The Muslim is not free to ascribe anything to accident or to blind fate. The Muslim regards earthquakes, pestilences, drought, and tragedy, as ordained by Allah (SWT). However tragic or painful, the Muslim accepts these events as effects of Allah (SWT), willed by Him for a good cause that may not be discerned presently. Being effects of Allah (SWT), the Muslim is never overwhelmed by them because he knows Allah (SWT), the Author of them, to be at once his Benefactor and his Protector. He, therefore, assumes them to be tests, ordained by Allah (SWT) to try him, calling for the greatest firmness, faith, and optimism in the final outcome.

Misfortunes that befall a Muslim or successes that may come his way only serve to galvanize him to still greater effort, to transform and to exert himself with hope and confidence, thereby reinforcing his strong relationship with Allah (SWT), the Creator of all beings, and helping him toward his ultimate goal. A Muslim faces life and its problems with patience and a deep sense of gratitude.

At times, the Muslim's daily struggles may not yield fruit, but this does not dishearten him nor deter him from exerting more effort. For he knows that, by doing so, he is conforming to the Divine Will and Ordainment to reform, to transform, to create, and to civilize through action, as well as to be ready to suffer, to sacrifice, and to face with fortitude all hardships for the cause of truth, justice, beauty, and goodness.

This aspect of the faith of Islam is precisely what humans need when faced with tragedy, especially when they are living in a spiritual void and are afflicted with psychological unrest in the face of challenges and the tragedies of life, whose deeper mysteries are beyond the reach of laboratories or institutions.

The ordaining by Allah (SWT) of this world as one in which causes are followed by their effects, where infinite interrelationships exist and bind everything together in a system of ends is itself, meant to provide a theatre for man's life and ethical endeavour. The theatre is not an end in itself; nor is it the property and exclusive domain of man. Since man is created for a life of service to His Creator, the world is His grant to him. Man's duty is, therefore, to work out the Divine patterns in it, while safeguarding it from deterioration and, indeed, improving it.

3. Subservience (*Taskhir*) of Creation to Man

Allah (SWT) has granted the world to man as a temporary gift and theatre. He has made everything in it subservient to him, i.e., capable of being used by man for his nourishment, enjoyment, and comfort. Such use may be immediate, as in the case of nourishment and enjoyment, or delayed, as when the forces of nature are utilized to produce the goods men need. Between the objects of creation and human use of creation there is a built-in concordance. The needs of humanity are built into creation, its objects being meant to serve those needs. The whole range of nature is capable of receiving the fruits of man's ability to build, of suffering change at his initiative, or experiencing transformation into any pattern man desires. Humankind can dry up the seas or harness the sun, move the mountains, and cultivate the deserts, or lay the whole world to waste. Man can fill the world with beauty and enable everything to prosper or fill it with ugliness and destroy everything. The subservience of creation to man knows no limits. Allah (SWT) has willed it this way. The causal and finalistic interconnections of the objects of creation are the substance of this subservience, which would be futile and meaningless without them. If man could not depend upon causes to bring about their effects or the means not to be good for the ends, he would quickly lose interest in creation and give up any attempt to transform it into the ought-patterns revealed by Allah (SWT). The Kantian notion, "You should, therefore, you can," which is the first principle of the metaphysics of ethics, is a Muslim axiom, first and best expressed by the Qur'anic principle, "Allah does not place a burden greater than one can bear" (Qur'an, 2: 286). Without this necessary implication, the universe would be either an inert, immovable, and unchangeable world or a world for fools. Certainly, it is not inert nor is it a world for fools. It is, in fact, a gift to man from his Creator as His vicegerent on this earth: "Behold, your Lord said to the angels, 'I will create a vicegerent on earth'" (Qur'an, 2:30).

C. Unity of Truth and Unity of Knowledge

Reason may certainly have its illusions and aberrations as well as its uncertainties. Its capacity for self-criticism protects it to a fair degree, but wherever ultimate truth and reality are concerned, its human predicament requires corroboration by the infallible source of revelation. Once the question of the first or ultimate principles are settled, then reason acquires new vigour with which it can overcome the problems confronting it. Its basic presuppositions must all be probably certain. Some are so by self-evidence; others are the common experience of humanity at large. There are others, however, that are capable of ought-necessity only, i.e., they are capable of being perceived as true only by those who have the requisite degree of wisdom or maturity of religious or ethical vision and who are, on that account, expected to see the reality as it is. Hence, recognition of such truths and values may not be mathematically universal but requires a different kind of necessity - an ought-to-be necessity. Where reason does not enjoy probable certainty, the light of faith can provide this certainty and even cast illuminating light on all other presuppositions, thereby supporting, with additional certainty, the whole worldview built upon them. The light of faith is definitely epistemological and is the consequence of reasonableness, not its opposite. Between it and the probably certain presuppositions of reason, there is affinity, harmony, correspondence, and complementarity. In Islam, unlike totally dogmatic religions, faith is never irrational in its role and contribution. It does not stand above reason, just as reason does not stand above faith. The perception of reason and faith as diametric opposites and of man as having to choose between them is the antithesis of the Islamic position.

Concerning the theory of knowledge, the position of Islam may best be described as based upon the unity of truth. This unity devolves from the absolute unity of Allah (SWT) and is convertible with it. Al Haqq ("The Truth") is one of the names of Allah (SWT).

Since Allah (SWT) is the One and Only Lord, as Islam affirms, truth cannot be equivocal. Allah (SWT) knows the truth, and, in His Revelation, He tells it as it is. What He conveys in the revelation cannot be different from reality, since He is the Creator of all reality as well as of all truth. The truth, which is the object of reason, is embodied in the laws of nature. These are the patterns of Allah (SWT) in creation. They are His Sunan, which are constant and unchangeable and, hence, are possible to discover, to establish, and to use for the benefit of humanity. Besides proclaiming Allah's (SWT) existence and creation, revelation provides instruction about the world, giving the very same laws of nature or Divine patterns in accordance with which the universe runs. Obviously, there can be no truer disclosure or rendering of these laws or patterns than by their Maker and Author. Theoretically, therefore, there can be no discrepancy. This logical equivalence of reason, truth, and reality with the facts of revelation is the most critical principle epistemology has ever known. This equivalence is based upon three principles underlying all Islamic knowledge.

First, the unity of truth prescribes that no claim on behalf of revelation may be made that counters reality. The propositions that revelation is supposed to teach must be true, i.e., they must correspond to reality and agree with it. It is inconceivable that Allah (SWT) may be ignorant or that He may seek to cheat or misguide His creatures. Therefore, His statements, expressly provided to guide and instruct, cannot oppose reality. Wherever an apparent variation from reality occurs, the Muslim is rightly cautioned by the doctrine of unity of truth to reconsider his understanding of revelation. This doctrine guards him against over-hasty interpretation, exaggerated allegorical interpretation and exegesis, and the acceptance of any material of any esoteric (*batin*) nature that is arbitrarily assumed on someone's personal authority. The meanings of Islamic revelation are eternally anchored in two solid rocks: Arabic lexicography and syntax, which have remained unchanged since the revelation of the Qur'an, and reality. This is why Qur'anic revelation has known no hermeneutical problems as such. All exegetical issues have revolved around questions of lexicography and syntax or excellence of understanding, correct thinking, experience, and profundity of knowledge.

Second, the unity of truth prescribes that no contradiction, difference or variation between reason and revelation is ultimate. It categorically affirms that there is an over-arching principle, fact or understanding that can solve the contradiction. When one investigates nature and attempts to discover the patterns of laws of the Creator in the universe, it is certainly possible to make mistakes, to fall under illusion, and to think one has grasped the truth while being in error. This would create discrepancy between revelation and reason. The unity of truth rejects such discrepancy as illusory and demands that the inquirer reconsider and reinvestigate the data. The cause of the discrepancy may well be in the findings of science or reason, in which case it would be salutary to have the investigator reexamine the relevant data. And the discrepancy may well be in the investigator's understanding of revelation, in which case it would be equally salutary to suggest a review of data. Such a re-examination in the light of the principle of unity of truth will unravel the truth and rectify perceptions, thereby removing the hypothetical contradiction between revelation, reality and its conception.

Third, the unity of truth and the laws of nature with the patterns of the Creator, prescribe that no inquiry into the nature of creation is infinite. No matter how much or how deeply we may come to know of these inquiries, there will always be more of them to discover. Hence, openness to new evidence and persistence of the quest are necessary characteristics of the Islamic mind that accepts the unity of truth. A critical attitude toward all human claims and an active search which is never ultimately conclusive, for the laws of nature, are at once necessary conditions of Islam and of genuine science. Under this view, the strongest conclusion is always tentative, valid only until new evidence has questioned, refuted, or verified it. The highest wisdom, the most certain pronouncement the human mind attains, must always be followed with the affirmation, "Allah knows better!" (*Allah aʿlam*).

D. Unity of Life

1. The Divine Trust (*Amānah*)

In a passage of the Qur'an, Allah (SWT) says: "And when (after creating heaven and earth) Allah told the angels that He was about to create a vicegerent and to assign him to the earth, the angels pleaded: 'Would You place on earth (persons) who will do evil and shed blood while we praise and adore You constantly?" Allah replied: 'I have an ulterior purpose which you do not know?

Having created Adam, Allah (SWT) taught him the names of all things, showed him to the angels, and asked them to name the things of nature. They could not and answered, 'Praise be to You. We know only what You have taught us. Yours is the Knowledge and the Wisdom.' Allah (SWT) asked Adam to tell the names, which he did Then Allah (SWT) asked the angels to prostrate themselves to Adam" (Qur'an, 2:30-34). In other passages concerning the creation of man, Allah (SWT) said: "We offered our trust to the heavens and the earth and the mountains. But they withdrew and feared to accept it. Man, however, agreed to carry it" (Qur'an, 33:72). "I have only created jinn and mankind that they may serve Me" (Qur'an, 51:56).

"Blessed be He in Whose hands is dominion, and He over all things has power. He Who created death and life, that He may try which of you is best indeed." (Qur'an, 67:1-2). The foregoing passages of the Qur'an answer for all time the question of whether or not man's being has a reason that explains it. Islam affirms and emphasizes that man has a reason for existence- to serve Allah (SWT).

The Divine Will is of two types. The first is destiny, which is realized necessarily, such as the Divine patterns upon which creation runs. These patterns are the laws of nature. They are immutable, and their fulfilment is cosmic. In addition to revelation, they may be known by reason. Allah (SWT) enjoined upon man to seek them, to understand them, to establish them as knowledge, and to utilize them to his advantage.

The second type is realized only in freedom, in conditions where both fulfillment and violation or nonfulfillment are distinct possibilities. These are the moral laws. They coexist with the laws of nature, i.e., they are always realized in a context of things, persons, and relations in the empirical world, but they belong to a different order from the empirical. These moral laws exist before any examination of them takes place. Whether or not they enter the real situation and become fulfilled therein depends upon that situation's fulfilment or upon their own specific requirements.

Moral laws demand the free exercise of their own particular requirements. They demand the free exercise of a personal will. Devoid of such will, "heaven and earth and mountains" are incapable of carrying the Divine trust (*amānah*). Only man carries it, for he alone is capable of such moral freedom. His capacity puts him above the angels, for they do not enjoy the freedom to obey and disobey. That, also, is why Allah (SWT) commanded the angels to prostrate themselves before man. Due to their lack of moral freedom, they are inferior to man. They are perfect and can only obey the orders of Allah (SWT). They praise and serve Him constantly and never disobey. Thus, the obedience of man is worthier than the obedience of angels, precisely because it is done by a person who has free will is capable of doing otherwise. When a person turns away from the way of evil, the way of the lesser good, the way of material, utilitarian, or selfish good and opts freely to do that which the moral law demands, he realizes a higher value. The moral life is a higher, superior, nobler, and greater kind of life. The higher part of the Divine Will does not enter history and become real unless human beings choose to realize it in freedom. The human being is, therefore, a cosmic bridge between the higher echelons of the Divine Will and historical reality. Human existence is of tremendous significance.

2. Vicegerency (*al Khilafah*)

Man's carrying the Divine trust constitutes his *khilafah* or vicegerency to Allah (SWT). His *khilafah* consists in fulfilling the moral laws, which include Islamic religious laws that seek to regulate ritual worship as well as moral laws that are quite this-worldly in their character and effect. The main corpus of religious or moral laws consists of actual practices of living, of being, and of doing. What they add to the actual practices is a quality, a perspective, a way of discharging those self-same practices. It is commonplace for human beings to desire, to grow and enjoy, to acquire and possess, to love, to marry and procreate, to seize and exercise power, etc. Islam wishes these activities to continue. It does not condemn them or wish them to stop. All it seeks is to have humankind enter into these actions with the right motivation and to perform them in a straightforward way. The right motivation is for them to be willed for the sake of Allah (SWT), and the straightforward way is to do them justly and righteously, to have them bring about their utilitarian or moral objective without entailing any undesirable, unjust or immoral consequences.

The aforementioned unity follows from the fact that Islam exemplifies the unity of Creation; it does not separate the sacred or religious from the secular. In its view, there is one reality only-not two-as in the case of religions that bifurcate life into a sacred sector and a secular sector. Nothing is, as such, sacred except Allah (SWT). Islam regards everything as creaturely, not sacred; and it assumes it to be good since it is Allah's (SWT). It is the manner in which we do what we do that fulfils or does not fulfil the religious or moral requirements. When what we do fulfils the moral requirement, it is good; when it does not, it is evil. Therefore, human deeds alone, could be good or evil, virtuous, or vicious, depending upon whether they bring about justice, righteousness, beauty, happiness, or otherwise.

To be religious, however, does not mean to withdraw from the usual processes of life nor to perform deeds that are utterly devoid of utility. The whole matter of religion is a quality of the very practices of living. On this account, Islam remains embedded in all the vicissitudes of life and history. There is neither piety nor virtue, and certainly no Islam, outside of these processes. Christianity and Buddhism may regard religion as something removed from the processes of life and history. They may prescribe self-mortification and asceticism, monkery, combat against, and even arrest of those very processes. They do so because, in their view, the normal life and history stand condemned as evil and doomed. Christianity, for example, believes creation is "fallen", "evil", and "hopeless" and prescribes faith and the imitation of Christ as salvation from them. Likewise, Buddhism believes creation is evil (tanha), full of nothing but pain and suffering, and prescribes self and life denial as salvation from life and history. Islam denies such axioms. In Islam's view, creation is good, brought about by Allah (SWT) for a good purpose; namely, that it may be affirmed with devotion to Him and justice to mankind. Involvement in the manifestations of creation is at the root of Islam's view of man. Allah (SWT) has appointed him to achieve two objectives. First, humans should transform creation into the Divine patterns, i.c., to rearrange its materials so as to make them fully and beneficially serve human needs, which are material (food, shelter, comfort, procreation) as well as moral, intellectual, and aesthetic. Second, in the very act of transforming creation, humans need to give substance to ethical values by choosing to enter into those acts of transformation in an ethical way, i.e., in a way that fulfils the requirements of devotion to Allah (SWT) and justice to mankind.

The content of the Divine *amanah* and, therefore, of *khilafah*, is the development and establishment of culture and civilization. To institute peace and assurance of life and property, and to organize humans into an ordered society that is capable of producing, processing, storing, and distributing food to all in adequate quantities and quality are a part of *amanah*. To provide shelter, warmth, and comfort, communication, and case, and to build and make available the tools necessary to realize these goals are part of *amanah*. Finally, to furnish opportunities for education and self-realization, for creation and aesthetic enjoyment are all part of *amanah* which, together, form the core content of *khilafah*. It is equivalent to making culture and civilization, to affirming and promoting life and the world. Allah (SWT) commands all this to be done and declares it to be the very reason for His creation of the world. The Divine ulterior motive in all this is that humans may realize their highest will and prove themselves ethically worthy by doing it. They can do so by entering into their ordinary routines of action for His sake and by maintaining the balance of justice throughout their actions.

Rightly, Muslims understand *khilafah* as directly political. Tae Qur'an repeatedly associated *khilafah* with establishing political powers: "We made you guardians and vicegerents [*khulafa*] in the land after them, so that we might see how you act" (Qur'an, 10:14). With the realization of peace and security, "Allah has promised to those of you who believe and do righteous deeds that He will surely make them [*khulafa*] in the earth as He made those before them [khulāfa'], and that He will surely establish for them their religion (way of life), which He has chosen for you, and that He will surely give them security in exchange for their fear" (Qur'an, 24:55). In another example, Allah (SWT) revealed, "He [Müsā] said: It may be that your Lord will destroy your enemy and make you *khulafa'* in the land, to try you by your deeds" (Qur'an, 7:129).

Political action, i.e., participating in the political process as in the election or confirmation (*bayah*) of the ruler, giving continual counsel and advice to the chief of state and his ministers, monitoring their actions, criticizing, and even impeaching them-all these are both desirable and prime religious and ethical duties. Failure to perform such duties, as the Prophet (SAAS) said, is to lapse into *jahiliyah* ("state of uncivilization"). The Prophet (SAAS) said: "You must enjoin good and forbid evil and punish the unjust for his injustice and compel him to accept the truth or restrict him to what is right, or Allah will estrange your hearts, turning you away from one another." To be part of the politico-economic body of Islam is integral to the faith of Islam. Abū Bakr and the *ashāb* (companions of the Prophet, RAA) fought those who wanted to secede from the state while maintaining their faith, regarding them as apostates rejecting the whole of Islam. Islam prohibits withdrawing from the political process or from culture and civilization building. Islam regards them as the very business of religion. This makes it all the more unintelligible as to why the Muslim masses distance themselves from the political process. The same is true of the requirement for peace and security.

Every Muslim must feel secure in his life, property, personal honour, and place in society. Fulfilling this requirement is the prime Islamic societal imperative. To this end, Islam requires that every Muslim be politicized, (i.e., awakened, organized, and mobilized) to seek fulfilment of this objective in his own person as well as in the persons of his family members, neighbours, and all fellow Muslims: "For them is security and they are guided right" (Qur'an, 6:82).

3. Comprehensiveness

The will of Islam to build culture and civilization is comprehensive, as it must be if it is meant seriously. This comprehensiveness is the foundation of the *Shari'ah.* Every aspect of human life is affected by the *Shari'ah,* which constitutes the relevance of Islam to it. This relevance may be legally binding, as in the Shariah's *wājibāt* and *muharramat* (duties and prohibitions), or unbinding, as in its categorizations of *mandüb* (recommended), *makrüh* (reprehensible), and *mubah* (permissible), variations of what is and is not acceptable. But nothing escapes Islam's relevance. True, the area of the *mubāh* is wide. Its width is not a sign of Islam's irrelevance but rather, is a sign of its fall outside the realm of strict enforcement, whether coercively, as in the case of the *wajib* and *harām*, or by moral authority, as in the case of the *mandub* and *makrūh*. Beyond that realm stands the realm of culture and lifestyle, which is just as important in Islam as that of strict enforcement. In fact, strict enforcement depends upon proper acculturation, which is its presupposition and without which it is unthinkable. Nothing is enforceable to which the masses have not been already acculturated, of which they are not already convinced.

It is, therefore, the duty of the Muslim thinker to Islamize, i.e., to define and apply the relevance of Islam to every single item in human living. The Qur'an has already done so in a number of areas of human activity, which normally have been assigned the status of "soft enforcement" or neutrality, e.g., greeting, using a soft voice, knocking on a door before entering, exiting quickly (as a guest) after dining, kindness to parents and elders, etc. The Prophet (SAAS) did his best to perfect the application by his teaching and example in the areas of how to eat and drink, to keep clean, to procreate, to treat one's neighbour, etc. Islam had instituted a style of life in the early period by elaboration or extension of these Qur'anic and Sunnatic directives. Today, this lifestyle needs to be redefined, recrystallized, and complemented to extend to those activities that were not known or common then, or the earlier directives need to describe how to apply those areas that modernity raised from the status of luxury or marginality to that of necessity. For example, the areas of social intercourse, travel and transportation, recreation, audio- visual arts, and mass communication, are especially in need of such extension of coverage by the relevance of Islam.

E. Unity of Humanity

Being the unity of the Creator, the Divine Unity must have absolutely the same Creator-creation relationship to all humans. The converse of this relation is that all humans must have absolutely the same creation relation to the Creator, different only in degrees of righteousness. Insofar as their being is concerned, they cannot exist as ultimately plural without this plurality implying an equal plurality in the Creator. Certainly, humans can and do have different characteristics such as race, colour, physical build, personality, language, and culture. But none of these characteristics can have ontological value, i.e., constitute the person it qualifies as a different being. None of them can affect the person's creaturely status before Allah (SWT). Their value remains superficial to the person's being the creature of Allah (SWT). Determining the personality or conduct of the possessor based upon a person's ethnic characteristics may very often bring about his moral felicity or ruin. These characteristics never determine ethical outcome and are never final or ultimate, for it cannot be an axiom that a person with any imaginable combination of such characteristics is morally worthy or unworthy. The inner core is constitutive of the person's being and must therefore remain, to the extent required, free of these characteristics-both capable of using their determinative power as well as of doing otherwise, i.e., of channelling their causal efficacy to other ends.

The foregoing argument is the reason underlying the Divine statement of the Qur'an: "O People, we have created you [all] of a single pair, a male and female; and We have constituted you into tribes and nations that you may know one another. Nobler among you in the estimate of Allah is the more virtuous" (Qur'an, 49:13). Perhaps the first and most obvious characterization of, and the first means of differentiation among humans, is belonging to one gender or another, to a certain tribe or nation, or to one ethnicity or another. The second set of obvious characterizations are language, physiognomy, intelligence, dexterity, and body strength, which are less fixed at birth and more apt to undergo change. The third include the readily changeable characteristics of personality that constitute the virtues and vices from wisdom and knowledge, piety, and patience, to ignorance and foolishness, faithlessness and rebellion. All these constitute the human personality and lifestyle, at least as its foundation. The rest of the personality and lifestyle is what develops out of habit and judgment, tendency and temperament, reputation, history, and tradition of that personality through the accumulation of its own deeds. All of these characteristics contribute to determining the human person. But they differ widely, from predetermination before birth and hence immutability, to acquisition in various stages of life, and then, to growth and development, or change and withering away.

Humans are most apt to mistake the values of these characteristics and the nature of the roles they play in the life of the person for the essence of the person. In history, no other human facts have determined the judgment of persons and groups more than the first order of characteristics, namely, gender and ethnicity. And, yet these are the most innocent because they are the least dependent upon moral decision and action, the least susceptible to change. In most cases, their immediacy and obviousness mislead judgment to take them as ontic and to differentiate and discriminate on their basis. That is why the Qur'an picked them as the first identifiers, necessary and unchangeable signs of the work of Allah (SWT), created by Him merely for the purpose of identification. They are to be regarded solely as a "passport" or "identity card", saying absolutely nothing about the moral character or value of the carrier. This is the meaning of the verse (Qur'an, 49:13) quoted above if its terms are taken literally. If the term "know" is taken figuratively, then the Qur'an would be telling us that gender and ethnic characteristics were created by Allah (SWT) so that humans could find in them mutual complementarity and cooperation.

All humans are, therefore, one and the same; this is the basis that forms the groundwork of Islam's universalism. All humans are one in the eye of Allah (SWT) except as their deeds distinguish them in moral virtue, in cultural or civilizational achievement. If these deeds are hampered because of pre-emptive, culturally limiting circumstances, it is a moral duty to alter and remove those culturally limiting circumstances in order to develop a new, healthy set of circumstances, which is always possible. The door to such alteration is never closed. On the other hand, where a person is judged because of these immutable characteristics, a mortal crime, namely, chauvinism, is committed. The implications of such a crime are ominous: both the unity of humanity and Divine unity are violated. Nothing is more odious to Allah (SWT) than shirk (associationism or polytheism); and chauvinism implies nothing less than shirk. Religion and all sorts of causes have been paraded as the source of various conflicts among groups of humans. In reality, nearly all conflicts among groups are ultimately reducible to chauvinistic decisions made upon the basis of the immutable characteristics of a so-called "enemy". With chauvinism, of which racism and nationalism are commonplace expressions, Islam can have no compromise. The conflict between them is insoluble, and the damage that chauvinism inflicts upon the human spirit, whether as subject or object of discrimination, is irreparable.

To condemn chauvinism, as Islam does, is not to condemn the basic elements of patriotism. Patriotism signifies the attitude of love and endearment, of appreciation of the life and value of the group, of self-preparation to undergo any exertion or sacrifice, including laying down one's life for the defence of one's land and people. As such, these basic elements of patriotism are not an evil but, rather, are a positive good enjoined by Islam as long as they do not lead to injustice and tyranny and do not become a form of chauvinism. It is both a religious and ethical duty to love and serve, to defend one's people and land against aggression and injustice.

Chauvinism, however, is far removed from patriotism. Its essence is to assume the advantage of the ethnic entity as the ultimate criterion of good and evil; and its most common expression is to hold the ethnic entity superior to mankind because of the image characteristics of its members, to regard and pursue that illusory advantage at the cost of any other. It is because chauvinism makes such assumptions that it is possible for it to command the absolute loyalty of the adherent. The claim it makes is the claim of ultimate reality. The committed chauvinist, whether Jew, German, French, or Russian, genuinely assumes the Jewish People, Germany, France, or Russia to be ultimate realities constituting ultimate criteria of good and evil. What Zionism built in the psyche of the Jewish people; what Hegel, Fichte, Nietzsche, and other Romantic thinkers built in the psyche of the German people as to what is "Deutschland"; what Rousseau, Fustel de Coulanges, and others built in to the psyche of the French people as to what is "la Nation" or "la France", was nothing short of a mystique that bloated them into something approximating the ultimate reality of religious faith. The pride and inspiration that those mystical entities command and the moving appeal that they exercise upon the heart and imagination of the adherent are, indeed, those of a reality that is mysterious, tremendous, fascinating, absolute, transcendent, and ultimate.

A Muslim believes the exact opposite of this conception of ultimate reality, precisely because the Muslim perception of Allah (SWT) is that He is absolutely the only God of all, the premise that necessitates his assumption of the unities referred to above as well as the unity of humanity. A Muslim nationalist or racist is, therefore, a contradiction in terms; and the Muslim who claims commitment to nationalism is either a *munafiq* (hypocrite), a *zindīq* (atheist), a non-Muslim pretending to be one, or one whose commitment is so superficial that it cannot withstand the lure of personal advantage. This is also the reason why the careers of the overwhelming majority of the so-called committed Muslim nationalist leaders have left much to be desired in the way of consistency, fidelity to the professed ideal, and moral integrity.

In modern times, knowledge of man has nearly all been based upon ethnicity as the ultimate definition of humanity; and knowledge of society has been based upon ethnicity as the ultimate ground of social order and organization. The universalism of the Enlightenment was never given a chance to be implemented before it was repudiated in favour of the chauvinistic approach of Romanticism. Indeed, the universalism of the Enlightenment was theoretical and suspicious, considering that, even in the hands of the prince of the movement, Immanuel Kant, the various peoples of mankind were graded as superior and inferior on the basis of traditional European prejudices and the innate characteristics of Asians, Africans, and Europeans. Romanticism swept over the entire

West; wiped out every trace of rationalist or Christian universalism; and provided the greatest impetus for the humanities, the arts, and the social sciences. Man was defined by the Romantic thinkers as a function of facts, faculties, and forces that spring and nourish themselves from a land mystically conceived, from a race or people or blood mysteriously standing in an infinite dimension of time, and from a tradition the roots of which are infinitely deep and extend in both space and time. Furthermore, these are understood not by reason but, rather, are grasped by feeling, immediate experience, and intuition. Their most eloquent and most clear expression is to be found in the arts, especially in music, painting, and literature. After conceding the point to its detractors that religion is irrational and arbitrary and of the same nature as "illusion" and "opium", Romantic thinkers, notably Schleiermacher, reconceived religion as founded solely upon the ineffable experience of the adherent, i.e., his personal feeling.

The Western humanities continued to speak of "man" and "humanity". But, in their Romanticized understanding, these terms denoted Western man and Western humanity. If they did not exclude the billions of "blacks", "browns", and "yellows" of Africa, Latin America, and Asia, it counted them only as approximations of humanity that could be colonized, exploited, and used for the welfare of Western humanity. The West thought these billions of people certainly ought to be studied; but they should be studied only as specimens of an age that the West once underwent and, thus, contribute to the Western man's historical "evolutionary" understanding of himself.

Chauvinism is internally divisive; for it is always possible to find, within any defined group, subgroups that reveal a greater concentration of innate characteristics than the larger group. Such a "fact" could then furnish the basis for a smaller group to call itself an ethnic entity endowed with a stronger particularism. Hence, Romanticism separated the Westerners from the rest of the world, with which they were coming into more intensive contact because of the development of industry and transportation and divided the West into mutually hostile and competitive nations, each seeking its "national interest" as if it were the criterion of all good and evil. The nations of the West learned from and readily accepted the findings of one another. The Romantic insights, analyses, and expression of one nation were quickly acknowledged as true of another and then adopted and applied as if they were its own.

The Western social sciences-history, geography, economics, political science, sociology, and anthropology-were all developed under the impetus provided by Romanticism. All of them, each in its own way, were based upon the chauvinistic view that the nation or ethnic entity, in its well-defined geography and demography yet infinite and woozy history, was the ultimate unit of analysis and value. When they spoke of "society" or "social order", they meant their own national unity or order.

Some are quite frank and open, while others are not so explicit; but, in their eyes, Romantically-based national chauvinism is still one of the most important and fundamental suppositions even if it is not mentioned explicitly.

What are known today as political science, geography, and history can only conceive of the world as a satellite to the West, a world revolving around England, America, France, Germany, or Italy as its heart and core, depending upon the author and place of publication. In its earlier stages, Western economics was impertinent enough to claim for itself the status of a universal science. But it was put back in its place as a Western analysis of a Western nation by the arch-Romanticists and chauvinists of Europe-the Nazis. The same bombastic claims made on behalf of the discipline by Karl Marx were denied in practice by Lenin and Khrushev. Their regime, however, has not yet permitted a statement to this effect to appear in print; but it allowed a fair measure of chauvinistic declarations, in this case national-socialistic, to be included in the new U.S.S.R. constitution of 1398 AH / 1978 AC.

Finally, anthropology is the boldest of all. In its view, "humanity" means ethnicity and is logically equivalent to and convertible with it. In the last two centuries, its effect has been to whip humankind into a frenzy of ethnocentric consciousness by singling out one subgroup after another, constructing for it an ideology and axiology out of that group's innate characteristics or by declaring to be innate and particular to one ethnic group whatever is being advocated. Instead of identifying and emphasizing what is universally human, anthropology's whole concern is to identify, to develop and to blow out of proportion the particular.

Islam rejects the negative attitude of ethnocentricity. However, it recognizes the family as the constitutive unit of social order and buttresses its extended form with legislation regarding inheritance and dependence to allow the largest possible family membership to eat from the same kitchen. The purpose of this buttressing is to encourage Muslims to live in close proximity to one another, preferably under the same roof, where the members of the extended family can mutually support their social, emotional and mental health and well-being. Beyond the family, Islam recognizes not the nation nor the ethnic group but, rather, all humanity-the universal social order. Nothing stands between the two circles of family and humanity. By themselves, they constitute all there is to the social order. Man's membership in this order is Islam's concern in the social sciences. Islam regards Human groupings between the family and humankind, namely, the country or region, the people or nation, as purely an administrative unit that is absolutely irrelevant to the definition of good and evil, to the interpretation and application of the Shari'ah. The arts, the humanities, and the social sciences of the modern West must, therefore, be totally recast. They must be given a new foundation of first principles that are concordant with the universalism of Islam. And they must receive from the Islamic thinker a new axiology, viz., Islamic values and ends, as ultimate objectives for guiding social research.

F. The Complementary Nature of Revelation (*Wahy*) and Reason (*'Aql*)

The Muslim's understanding of the nature between revelation and reason is a tenet that is based upon Islamic ontology. Allah (SWT) has gifted man with reason, which is the tool required to know the world around him, to utilize it in satisfying his needs and in shouldering his responsibilities as a vicegerent. On the other hand, Divine revelation is meant to guide man toward knowledge of the aims of righteous life, of the definition of its responsibilities, and of ascertaining its components. Revelation enlightens man, despite his limited mental powers, about metaphysical concepts, about relationships in the whole universe and on earth, and about the complexities of human and social interactions and concepts. All of these are indispensable for endowing the human mind and will with the power to account for liabilities and for guiding man's energies and behaviour in accordance with his aims in life. Thus, revelation and reason are both complementary and essential for righteous life on earth.

If reason has existed since the birth of humanity, so have Divine revelation and Divine messages. Divine revelation represents the Divine call to man for believing in truth, justice, righteousness, and constructive toiling on earth. On the Day of Judgment, the good and the evil done by every soul will be rewarded and penalized from the greatest accomplishments to the smallest misdeeds.

Thus, there is no sense in the assumption of contradiction between revelation and reason. They are both meant to complement each other in human life, to help man to realize his aims in it and to shoulder his responsibilities. It is important for us to assess correctly their relationship if we are to know the place of each within the framework of the Islamic personality, thought, and conduct. This is essential for us to realize the complementary nature of revelation and reason and to bypass any illusion of contradiction between the two.

The human mind, despite its place and potential in human life, is dependent upon accumulating, processing, and deducing knowledge and experience to perform its functions. Through chosen messengers, Divine revelation endows reason with concepts of cosmic relationships, the place of man in Creation, his mission on earth, the laws governing his human and social relationships that are essential to guide his conduct and to help him realize his aims in life.

Reason will be well-balanced only when it submits to the guidance of revelation as to the ultimate aim of existence. Muslims went astray when they utilized reason in other than its correct ways and when, under the influence of Greek thought, they depended upon erroneous guess work in matters of Divinity and such issues as "fate" and "destiny", which had no guidance from revelation.

To the Muslim, the mainstay of this complementary nature and the cornerstone of the structure of his personality is the fact that revelation has set the framework within which reason is to function toward realizing man's purposes in his earthly life with all possible seriousness and sincerity. Reason is never to function toward the exertion of fruitless, irresponsible efforts.

A major benefit to all people would be for Muslim thinkers to comprehend and to outline the infinite ways in which reason and revelation can complement each other and how, exactly, this cooperation can be applied to the everyday decision-making processes of life.

Chapter V: Agenda of the Institute

A. Agenda Objectives

Although the agenda discussed in this book represents, in essence, the Institute's actual course of future action and the Institute's intention to implement as great a part of it as possible, it remains a comprehensive general plan. Any sincere member of the Muslim Ummah or any of its academic or cultural organizations interested in resolving this academic-cum-ideological problem is welcome to participate in its accomplishment. It is a plan for Islamizing knowledge; for reforming contemporary modes of Islamic thought; for reviving its methodology; and for restoring its dynamic originality, creativity, and ability to contribute. As such, its success does not depend exclusively upon the efforts of the Institute. To achieve its implementation, every sincere Muslim, indeed, all concerned Islamic organizations struggling to reestablish Islamic order and civilization, may cooperate with the Institute for the guidance and general welfare of the human race in order to discharge our collective duty in this life as Muslims. The aims of the Institute's plan for the Islamization of Knowledge are as follows:

(1) To create awareness in the Ummah of the crisis of ideas. This involves enlightening the Ummah about the place and methodology of the crisis of Islamic thought in the perspective of its cultural and civilizational existence.

(2) To foster a deeper understanding of the nature of the crisis of ideas in contemporary Islamic thought, its causes, and its solutions.

(3) To define the critical relationship between the failure of Islamic thought and its methodology; the current absence of the Ummah as a civilization; and its failure to succeed as a free, progressive, and prosperous nation.

(4) To work toward reviving the ideologies of the Ummah, reinvigorating and gradually redeveloping its methodology, and elucidating its viewpoints and its intimate relationship with original Islamic goals.

(5) To work for adopting and incorporating comprehensive Islamic methodology in the fields of social sciences and the humanities, as well as to foster and fund scientific studies in actual individual and social life conditions.

(6) To implement the requisite steps to allow the developing contemporary Islamic culture and methodology to avail themselves of the fountains of Islamic principles and legacy, as well as of modern sciences and knowledge, by making them accessible and digestible to Muslim students.

(7) To provide help in researching, studying, and working on the methodology and its presentation, with a view toward elucidating Islamic concepts and intellectual outlook and toward laying the foundation for the evolution of Islamic social sciences and humanities.

(8) To prepare the requisite intellectual cadres to broaden the field of Islamization of knowledge through providing stipends for studies, providing academic supervision, and establishing academic programs of Islamic studies in all fields of contemporary social sciences and humanities.

B. Stages of the Agenda

The ultimate objective is to introduce the concept of "Islamization", discarding such notions as "westernization" and "modernization". This shall become a comprehensive Islamic and human concept, providing a cultural framework that is at once original and creative. It will be able to comprehend the potentialities of the age and to exploit them all in order to promote Islam's civilized and noble values. It is essential, therefore, that these efforts be directed into various parallel channels that are mutually related, thereby coordinating the efforts of the Institute with those of other scholars, thinkers, educated people, and Islamic academic organizations. These efforts must be well- organized and the cooperation of all those who are actively engaged in work and reform in various fields must be solicited. While priority is placed upon reforming confused thought and methodology, we must not underrate the importance of practical, organizational, and combative efforts being waged in various fields. All really sincere efforts should complement, rather than contradict, one another and should support the movement toward the true Islamic path.

The efforts toward rectifying Islamic thought, methodology, and knowledge demand work in the following fields and related channels.

1. Creation of Understanding and Awareness

Ideological reformation and Islamization of knowledge are not things that, once done, are thereafter no longer worried about or considered. Nor are they a problem that concerns only a limited number of people or their activities. The reformation of Islamic thought and the Islamization of knowledge call for consistent and persistent work in the life of the Ummah. In its present state, the Ummah is well able to resume its onward march, to grasp and develop its own potential, and to steer its course through the ever-changing new phases of existence.

The problem of knowledge and thought concerns a wide cross-section of people. It includes scholars, thinkers, the educated elements of the Ummah, and their leaders alike. All jointly erect its social edifice and work together for its revival. They partake of common benefits and work together and suffer for it, directing the efforts of the Ummah and determining its civilizational form. Therefore, the first step on the road to reformation and Islamization must be to educate and inform its prospective helpers and to position them in their respective places in its ranks so that they may be better able to appreciate its effects upon their works, academic undertakings, and intellectual endeavours. We must, therefore, address all scholars, thinkers, educated classes, leaders, and students through their diverse organizations, groups, clubs, and forums of Islamic media.

Such awareness cannot be created by just sending out personalized circular letters. The agenda must involve offering opportunities for such actions, programs, and preparation as may help serve the ideological cause and the Islamization of knowledge. An agenda objective should revive the spirit of inquiry and make use of the skills and efforts of Muslim intellectuals. It should allow for invitations to participate actively in various works and programs of reformation, development, education, and publication.

For this purpose, the Institute holds seminars and conferences and makes full use of the mass media, with special emphasis on publications. It seeks and endeavours to enlist the cooperation of all academic institutions and the mass media with a view to explaining the issues and elucidating their various aspects, inviting all members of the Ummah to participate and contribute.

The Institute has held a number of international conferences and academic seminars on various fields of knowledge. The Institute invites scholars and Muslim students to these seminars and seeks to organize permanent groups for creating awareness of the problems of Islamic thought and Islamization in all international centres of knowledge in general and in those of the Islamic world in particular. Likewise, the Institute is aware of the importance of a vigorous campaign involving mass media of communications to explain this problem and to consider its future course so that the scholars of the Ummah and its students may come to identify it as their own problem-a problem that should provide them with a framework for all their intellectual and academic work.

The Institute eagerly hopes to win the attention of leaders, thinkers, and academic organizations since they are better placed and can, through their ample resources, expand the sphere of the desired awareness of the problem to make the Ummah realize and appreciate its true dimensions. Thus, all its intellectual and academic efforts will be ultimately channelled into a new revivalist mode. The Institute looks hopefully to the day when the fruits of its work in conferences, seminars, studies, and publications will be fully realized, together with the achievements of other academic organizations and sincere workers who are tackling this problem. It hopes to present the rest of the Ummah with such noble patterns and alternatives that will be exemplary and will provide people with tangible models to emulate.

2. Crystallization of Islamic Thought, Concepts and Methodology

Resolving the crisis in Islamic thought is essential in order to realize the Islamization of knowledge and to release and divert the energies of the Muslim community toward improvement and progress. However, it cannot be effectively done without some preliminary academic work on elucidating Islamic thought to clarify its basic notions and to rectify its methodology. Therefore, it is imperative for the Institute (and, indeed, for anyone sincerely interested and concerned) to try to mobilize all the Islamic thinkers, scholars, and those qualified in both Islamic and Western knowledge to work in any specialized field of the Islamization of knowledge because there are few learned people of this category in the world today.

The Institute launched a special program for university teachers, scholars, and thinkers. This program provides the necessary support to help them spend their sabbatical leaves at the Institute in order to devote their time exclusively to research. Additionally, the Institute is trying to raise funds to support those scholars of outstanding merit and originality so that they can devote their time to certain topics. These combined efforts will, *in shaa Allah*, produce pioneer academic works that will guide and help others who are working in various fields toward the Islamization of knowledge.

The work on the crystallization of thought and reform of methodology is of fundamental importance. It involves a study of the contents of Islamic thought and methodology, as we know them today, and a need to present them with their basic issues recast into a perfectly integrated form with a new ability to relate to twentieth century issues. This will reinvigorate Islamic thought and methodology and restore to them their lost efficacy, allowing the Ummah to perceive them as a vibrant ideology and a certain and comprehensive methodology. The practical aids for all this will be decided in the light of the creed, norms, and concept of Islam, as enshrined in the Qur'an and Sunnah. Islamic ideology, as understood by the first generation of Muslims, will then play a new role-one that is similar to the one it played earlier and that will open up new horizons for the contemporary generation as it did with the first generation. This will allow them to deal with their world, to increase their energies, and to enhance their opportunities so that they may tackle the problems and the challenges that face them.

The pioneering efforts for crystallizing the contents of contemporary Islamic ideology and its methodology require that we master the fundamental principles of Islam, in the Qur'an, the Sunnah of the Prophet (SAAS), as well as the related sciences of *Shari'ah*, the Arabic language, and the early history of Islam. A thorough understanding of the problems of the present age, its sciences, its resources, and its challenges also are required. This can be achieved only by developing critical insight that is able to express itself in contemporary terms and that also is capable of confronting and solving contemporary issues and challenges. At the same time, it must explain the ideals, objectives, and basic stance of Islam concerning various important fields of life and contemporary knowledge. In addition to this, we should present a comprehensive and logical explanation of how and why the malaise that afflicted Islamic ideology and methodology over the past centuries, rendering them inadequate and inert, happened. This critical insight will also focus upon Islamic concepts and indicate what organizations, means, and academic, educational, and social reforms are necessary for bringing about a change in the present condition of the Ummah. This insight will reinstate Islamic ideology in its former role as the guiding force behind all the Ummatic efforts for civilization and transformation.

The crystallization of the basic principles of Islam and its distinct philosophy with respect to different fields, as well as its integrated academic methodology, are of prime importance in this first stage of revival and reformation. The Institute intends to realize these aims at the present stage by mobilizing the rare and scant intellectual energies and skills available. It is hoped that this overall philosophical and methodological vision will provide the scholars who are working in different academic fields with insight.

It is hoped that it will enlighten and help them to recast their special subjects of study in the framework of the beliefs, principles, values, and ideals of Islam and to advance, in all fields, the cause of what we have termed the Islamization of knowledge. If the efforts exerted are persistent and incessantly subjected to a process of adaptation and revision, they may make the vision brighter, clearer, and more comprehensive. Similarly, the continuous effort to improve its method of presentation and to develop its resources will help the Ummah in its onward march by developing its potential and by exploiting the opportunities to live up to the challenges of transformation and civilization.

3. Mastery of the Legacy

A. Plan Envisioned by the Institute: Mastery of the fundamental principles of Islam and the precious treasures of the legacy of the ancestors on the part of educated Muslims is the main pillar of the edifice of the Islamization of knowledge. No amount of present Ummatic striving can help promote the cause of construction, civilization, and transformation unless it is based, ideologically and methodologically, upon sound and firm bases. Even the presence of genuine understanding and knowledge of Islamic ideology and methodology may not be useless if confined to a small number of individuals within a community, who may have acquired their understanding through their own individual efforts under certain specific influences. For them to be beneficial to the Ummah, these individuals must emanate from the very being of the Ummah and its cultural make-up, converging and forming, as it were, a steady and powerful fountainhead of its Ummatic knowledge and lore, to enlighten and guide its students and educated members.

If Islamic culture and mastery of the fundamental principles of Islam and the precious treasures of the legacy remain confined to a few thinkers and scholars because of special environments in which they grew up or because of their mental process or their exceptional circumstances, that will not be of much help toward the objectives of the Islamization of knowledge or reformation of ideas.

To attain the goal of reformation and Islamization of knowledge, the means must, of necessity, be within easy reach of all the educated members of the community, forming a natural part of their fields of study and their academic faculties and educational methodologies. The single most important means of achieving the purity, firmness, and nobility leading to the Islamization of knowledge is the ability of the educated elements of the Ummah to have a firm grasp and command of the fundamentals of Islam and the precious treasures of the legacy.

The Institute's agenda to help educated Muslims to gain mastery over the fundamentals of Islam and the treasures of its legacy, thereby making them both easily accessible, consists of providing a broad outline of needed work, offering certain models, and then inviting scholars and academic institutions to come forward to help accomplish this stupendous task.

The requisite legacy, which must be classified and made easily accessible, falls into three categories. The first includes texts that enshrine the fundamental principles of Islam, which are the Qur'an and the Sunnah. The second consists of the traditions of the righteous ancestors, especially from among the Companions of the Prophet (SAAS), depicting their characters, thoughts, and practical methodologies. The third includes the entire thought-content of the scholars, reformers, and leaders of the Ummah over the centuries concerning various fields of knowledge. This is found in two subcategories. One consists of encyclopaedic works, which superimpose and touch upon almost all the branches of knowledge in excursus. Of these works, the most important ones are the commentaries on the Qur'an and Hadith. The other includes works that deal with certain specific topics or fields. Three of the most outstanding examples of this subcategory are the books, *Al Siyāsah al Sharīyah* (The Islamic Polity), *Al Ahkam al Sultānīyah* (The Rules of Governance), and *Kitab al Kash* (The Book of Earned Deeds).

It would be impossible to restore the purity of Islamic ideology, to master it, and to make it an integral part of the Ummatic consciousness, its being, its thought, its collective conscience, and its intellectual and civilizational role if the educational system of the Ummah and the sciences taught in it remained divorced from the fundamentals of Islam; namely, from the teachings of the Qur'an, the Sunnah, the Prophet's Sirah (the biography of the Prophet SAAS), and the history of his Companions, that explains and interprets them, and from the early history of Islam.

The agenda of the Institute concentrates upon realizing two academic objectives.

The First: providing the necessary means to facilitate classifying the legacy. This classification will be accomplished according to a method designed along the lines of contemporary social and human sciences and their important issues, in order to make it easy for scholars, thinkers, and other educated people working on contemporary sciences and social issues to refer to the legacy. This will allow them to easily conform their thinking to that of the legacy and to tackle the issues they may be dealing with in the light of the ideals and guiding principles of the legacy.

The facilitation of knowledge of the legacy requires that the means necessary for classifying the legacy be provided and, additionally, requires that a sound understanding of the legacy and of the process of working on the classified material be encouraged and promoted. This requires elucidating some aspects of the terminology of the legacy, recasting it in such moulds and forms as would be generally easy to understand. This is especially true in the case of the science of Hadith and its terminology.

To make work on the legacy practical, it is essential to present its terms in a uniform and clear manner to make them an easy vehicle for correctly understanding a text and for appreciating its significance and meaning.

Thc Sccond: to classify samplcs of thc works of thc lcgacy and to present them to scholars and academic bodies. This will facilitate their understanding and allow them to accomplish the classification of the vast number of selected legacy works, which embody the intellectual endeavours of innumerable minds of generations of the Ummah over the centuries. Such selected legacy works rightly deserve the attention of the scholars and researchers of the Ummah and should be republished in a classified and easily intelligible form. In addition to classifying sample studies, the Institute seeks to help researchers interested in the classification of the legacy by introducing and drawing attention to approximately 1,000 of the important encyclopaedic works of the legacy and by explaining the need to classify them.

B. An Encyclopaedia of the Legacy Works: The Institute's efforts in the field of making the legacy easily accessible will be published, *in shaa Allah*, in the form of an academic encyclopaedia that will provide the general requisite resources and samples in the manner detailed below:

1) Computer Utilization: This part deals with the means to facilitate a reclassification of the works of the legacy. It involves using computer technology and developing a coding system to categorize the materials of the basic sources of the legacy according to the various branches of contemporary knowledge, thereby allowing immediate access to and selection of material related to a particular subject in Islamic sources.

Using computers in this reclassification effort will make the procedure efficient and will conserve human effort. As a preliminary, the Institute has begun work on preparing the requisite computer coding system in research related to the reclassification of the legacy fields.

The use of this coding system, which will consist of key word classification, will make the work of the scholars simpler. It will be limited to a critical examination of the material provided by the computer and then either prepare it for publication or store it in the form of various programs on the legacy.

Obviously, a computer will be helpful in three ways: (1) by making research on legacy works easier by allowing immediate comparisons among various sources; (2) by making the extraction of academic material from the legacy concerning various fields and issues accessible through immediate cross- referencing; and (3) by helping scholars (since most of them are not computer programmers) store the classified academic material from the legacy in a form that will make it easier for other research workers to use.

It may be noted here that using computers to help facilitate classifying the legacy is not confined to setting up codes. It also requires developing an entire Arabic-language electronic structure for use in the classification effort.

The Institute has contacted certain manufacturing companies for help in developing such a system, which will initially require introducing such an Arabic computer system into the open marketplace. We hope this will be accomplished soon, and perfecting the coding system will follow in due course.

2) Terminology: The effort to make the terminology of the legacy and its sciences easily understood will primarily be undertaken in the following three fields:

(1) the sciences of Hadith, criticism of its text, chain of authorities, critical assessment of its narrators, and the terms used in it;

(2) the sciences of *fiqh* and its principles; and

(3) the methodology and terminology of Islamic history.

The purpose of all this is to prepare and to present such studies that will help standardize and facilitate the terminology of the legacy; explain its background in clear, intelligible, and coherent style; and make it easy for researchers, scholars, and thinkers to understand it, utilize it, and base their analogous judgments on it.

In the light of these studies and with the help of this new terminology, and equipped with an awareness and understanding of the historical background of a particular piece of the legacy and the methodology involved the task of the researchers and scholars will be made much simpler. It also will give them access to the genuine origins of the legacy.

3) Processed Samples of Legacy Texts: This part of the proposed encyclopaedia will contain classified anthologies of texts from references on the fundamental principles of the legacy and other encyclopaedic legacy works. It will introduce the classified texts and include a criticism in proper historical background, footnotes to explain and interpret the subject matter, terminology, and commentary. It will provide the essential indexes required to facilitate the use of any given material.

4) Introducing a Thousand Legacy Works: This part of the proposed encyclopaedia will include reviews of a thousand selected legacy works representing the genuine record of the earlier scholars and thinkers of the Ummah, while avoiding works that represent various forms of deviation, backwardness, excess, and extremism-the maladies that afflicted the Ummah and are responsible for its decline, loss of universal character, balance, serenity, and efficacy.

An introduction to each book will be prepared. It will provide the historical background, its author, his basic methodology; the age in which the author wrote and the main issues with which the work deals; its most prominent aspects, originality, or deficiencies; its sources of subject matter, methodology, and workmanship; and, additionally, other information that will be helpful to anyone wanting to edit and classify its contents.

5) Specialized Legacy Series: A series of specialized legacy works that cover different fields will be issued. Of these works, as we have explained earlier, some are encyclopaedic in nature and discourse on diverse subjects and fields at great length. All books of this kind must be revised and reclassified according to the contemporary scheme of knowledge and sciences. As to the books that deal with only one specific topic or field, the best and easiest solution will be to publish them just as they are along with helpful commentary to make their study simple and beneficial.

The Institute proposes, Allah (SWT) willing, to issue this series of legacy works as a complement to the Encyclopaedia of the Legacy. This series will explain the nature of the efforts needed to work on the legacy and how best to bring its contents within easy reach of present-day scholars, researchers, and educated people. The Institute hopes to be able, through the prospective Encyclopaedia, through other Institute publications, and through its support of the publications of other scholars and Islamic academic institutions, to present to educated Muslims a number of important specialized and unspecialized books along with critical and analytical studies. These publications will clarify the vision of the ancestors concerning their times, their methodologies, and how they reacted to the important issues of the age and its major trends; and how their vision moved them, how it reflected their civilizational achievements and their culture, how it found expression in their practice, behaviour, and life; and how this vision helped them to cope with the problems and the challenges that they faced.

By bringing the legacy within easy reach of educated Muslims, it is hoped that the Encyclopaedia will smooth the way for gaining the necessary knowledge that educated Muslims might need in any field of their interest. The Encyclopaedia swill follow an objective methodology, to which they are accustomed, and will give them access to the best of the legacy in the form of a collection of issues covering the main headings of any particular field of study. In this way, it will fill in the gaps in available knowledge, skilfully making up for lack of knowledge of with the language of the legacy and the keys to its treasures.

This methodological-cum-intellectual work in the field of the legacy, its classification, and its explanation will enable the educated and the scholars, Allah (SWT) willing, to find answers to these three important questions.

First: What is the contribution of the Islamic legacy, starting with the Qur'an and ending with the modern Muslim revivalist scholars, in dealing with the issues that modern knowledge and science pose?

Second: How does one reconcile or compare the contribution of the Islamic legacy with the achievements of modern science? And how far has the Islamic legacy broadened and expanded the vision and horizons of science? And what are the points of agreement, difference, or distinction between them? And in what ways is one deficient or inadequate compared with the others?

Third: What would be the best course for Muslims to adopt in mastering, reforming, and amending modern science in a manner to help realize the Islamic vision and its goals? And how must Islamic endeavours be directed to confront contemporary challenges; to rectify their weaknesses; to restate and reformulate the issues involved and, thereby, expand the horizons of the Islamic vision and render it the dominant civilizational vision of humanity at large, as willed by Divine Will for the human race of the earth?

4. Mastery of Contemporary Knowledge

Mastery of Islamic thought and a thorough knowledge and acquaintance with modern sciences are both necessary for the Islamization of knowledge. A distinguishing feature of the legacy in studies of social and physical nature is that they are the outcome of profound individual contemplation. In contrast, because of the impact upon it of the Islamic sciences and the Islamic indicative and empirical methodology, contemporary non-Muslim thought received new impetus for social and physical studies. Eventually, contemporary non-Muslim thought emerged from the stage of individual contemplation to a level of profound and organized study that employed certain standards and methodology and produced a large body of knowledge and numerous social, human, physical, and practical sciences, the benefits, and bitter fruits of which humanity has had experience in almost all spheres of life.

It was through this methodology and with the help of these sciences (especially in the fields of political, educational, economic, and military organization and technology) that the West achieved unprecedented successes in material civilization and was able to launch against the Islamic world a fierce political, economic, military, and cultural onslaught. The ferocity of this onslaught baffled the Muslims. They looked to the Western countries in search of a remedy for their ills, weakness, defeat, and sense of helplessness. And there they went to seek the knowledge and sciences of the Western nations to transform their own lives. But they remained as weak as ever; no matter how hard they tried, they failed to transcend modern science and to regain mastery. In their eagerness, generation after generation emulated the alien ways and manners of others, as if these ways and manners were a precious achievement in their lives.

One of the causes of these Muslim failures to attain their goal in this respect is that they accepted the new knowledge, science, and systems in a disjointed condition-as they were, without any critical appraisal, examination, or understanding of the ideals, norms, ideas, values, objectives and institutional make-up of the people responsible for developing these sciences. The disjointed approach and unimaginative methodology that Muslims adopted in acquiring the Western disciplines are responsible for their inability to produce any comprehensive critical studies. These studies could have helped them to understand the principles underlying Western thought, the spirit of Western civilization, its basic philosophy, its ideals, and the values that it embodies and reflects.

Muslims will never, under present conditions, be able to transcend these sciences or develop any creative faculty in them. They are bound to remain weak, backward, and unable to excel in any field of science or civilization, no matter how long they continue to dispatch the best of their sons and daughters to the Western metropolises.

Until the time that Muslims are able to arrest this weakness and to change the present distressing situation and until the time when they are able to develop the requisite intellectual prowess and creative genius, they have no option other than to acquire, understand and assimilate modern sciences and their creative potential in a moral perspective. To begin, this requires an ability on their part to understand, to grasp, and to make a critical objective study of Western civilization, its origins, ideals, philosophy, and accomplishments.

Neither partial acceptance nor outright frenzied rejection can be of use to Muslims in facing contemporary challenges. They must be able to exploit all the opportunities offered by modern civilization and, from there, move ahead toward what is far more comprehensive in its significance, purer and better in performance and accomplishment. However, this does not mean that, while studying the achievements of contemporary civilization and until Muslims are in a position to transcend it, they should endorse its propaganda and open their hearts and minds to its cultural invasion and welcome its alien colonialist hegemony. The process of gaining thorough acquaintance with this civilization and the effort to grasp its scientific and civilizational potential must take place within the right framework and show how deeply contemporary civilization is indebted to Islam and Islamic civilization. Current scientific and technological achievements are based upon the ideas, methodology, and skills that were borrowed from Muslims and were unknown prior to them. These achievements are truly a common heritage of the human race. Because Muslims are one of its architects, they are rightly expected to transcend it, to rescue it, and to guide its course afresh for improvement, progress, and growth. But, at the same time, they must be aware of the flaws and defects that science and technology have picked up while being developed by non- Muslims. These flaws and defects have tarnished Western thought, making any direct uncritical approach to it ungainly and harmful. Imitation and creedal contradiction, which might afflict our polity as a result of borrowing from non-Muslims without grasping the real significance of what we borrow, could all the more weaken us, leaving our lands and resources open to exploitation by aliens.

In order to help generate an overall critical approach toward contemporary Western civilization, the Institute is working on preparing a comprehensive survey of modern sciences, especially the basic social sciences and humanities. This survey will provide a brief account of each science and outline its main issues, methodology, and achievements. It also will list its important books, main sources, and important aspects of criticism in the eyes of some of its prominent scholars as well as from the viewpoint of Islam. This will provide a basic and comprehensive reference work which will give the Muslim scholar working in a specific field a critical insight into the subject at hand and which will increase the possibilities of intellectual prowess and independence that are essential for any intellectual progress and Islamic contribution to a discipline.

The Institute hopes to follow this up by issuing brief but comprehensive reports that will provide summaries of these studies. These summaries will present contemporary civilization with all its multifarious aspects and will assess its disciplines, its history, philosophy, origins, norms, and methodology in a critical and objective manner. Such brief studies will give the Muslim scholar and the ordinary educated Muslim a comprehensive and independent outlook on the subject, covering both its main issues and disciplines and, also, providing information on the issue of civilization and civilizational onslaught, reaffirming the individuality of Islamic academic endeavour, elucidating its stance, and reasserting its independent outlook.

For Muslim scholars to transcend the modern disciplines and to polish overall critical and objective understanding of contemporary civilization, they also must understand their own origins, Islamic values, ideals, and the essence of their ancestors' thoughts through the choicest treasures of the legacy. This is a fundamental condition and prerequisite to scholars' making any Islamic contribution or discharging any obligation regarding the Islamization of knowledge. It is essential for a scholar to be able to make any worthwhile intellectual and cultural contribution that is capable of expanding the horizons of human civilization and of giving man the power to deal with the diverse problems and dangers that overcast this world.

The agenda of the Institute, designed to enable the educated Muslim to transcend contemporary civilization, comprises the following steps:

(1) Preparation of three comprehensive surveys in every discipline, empirical or social, by three specialists

(2) Comparison of the three different surveys and preparation of one survey synthesizing all three.

(3) Preparation of a scientific file on the surveyed subject along with an introduction to the project and its targets. This will enable the Muslim scholar to transcend, to gain knowledge, comprehensiveness, independence of approach, and acquaintance with the fundamentals of Islamic criticism. The file will be distributed to the libraries of Islamic universities (approximately 180 to 200 pages). It will be reviewed and, if there is sufficient

demand, the dossier will be published. With respect to executing this common project, the Institute is ready to enter into agreement with other academic organizations for translation of the file into various languages in order to expand its sphere of impact.

(4) Examination of the file and preparation of a book that will cover certain portions of the subject while giving summaries of others. This book will be of a reasonable size (approximately 150 pages) to encourage its reading. Its purpose is not to cover artistic or technical details but, primarily, to promote a comprehensive and universal outlook in its readers. It should be equally useful for professional and other readers to acquire general acquaintance with the subject along with an understanding of the basis of Islamic criticism. The book will be published and translated.

(5) Urging of Muslim scholars to write critiques of the issues raised in these books, of their overall thought-content, and of their impact upon intellectual independence as part of the issue of the Islamization of knowledge.

(6) Preparation of an overall comparative study of Western civilization, tracing its origins, philosophical bases, ideals, and conceptions; its spatial and temporal characteristics; its general history; its achievements and methodology; and its Western and Islamic assessments. This will complement an introduction by explaining the objectives of the study, which include promoting comprehensive understanding and independence of approach; by identifying points of strength and weakness, utility, and temporal and spatial limitations of Western civilization; and by comparing and explaining the philosophy and meaning of Islamic civilization, its ideals and philosophical origins, and how they differ from Western civilization.

This study will be based upon existing works of Western disciplines and civilization in general. The study will be the substance and quintessence of the transformation and preparation of the Muslim intellect. It will be comprehensive and objective in its approach and will present the thought- content in the form of examples and well-defined, clear evidence from history. At the same time, it will expound views, mention accomplishments, and emphasize the ideological and aesthetic superiority of Islam and its impact upon Western civilization. It will explain the ideological revolution of the Western Renaissance, its ethics, material success, and why, though influenced and impressed by Islam, it refused to acknowledge its debt to Islam. Likewise, the study will underline the importance of determined adherence to the Islamic faith, ethics, and ideals as a basic condition for any civilizational progress, any right perspective, and any beneficial exploitation of the material successes of Western science and methodology. This study will be in an easily readable work, which also will be easy to render into other languages, Allah (SWT) willing.

5. Textbooks in Disciplines

The agenda of the Institute envisages the cooperation and help of various prominent scholars and organizations of the Ummah in elucidating the Islamic vision to pave the way for solid constructive work and to guide its future course in the right direction. The Institute seeks to achieve this purpose by presenting indispensable model works to Muslim scholars and educated Muslims to prepare them for the reformation of Islamic thought and to lay down the bases for Islamic social sciences and the Islamization of knowledge. This presentation will be in the form of card-catalogued samples of legacy works according to the classification scheme of each science of the fundamentals of Islam (the Qur'an, the Sunnah, and the works of the early righteous Muslims). It will include the best of the treasures of the legacy, thus establishing a relationship between educated Muslims and their traditional origins.

The Institute is in the process of preparing comprehensive critical studies of contemporary disciplines and civilization to enable the educated Muslim to transcend them in order to be intellectually and psychologically free.

Other than work in the two fields of elucidating vision and assessing contemporary Western civilization, the Institute proposes to authorize the preparation of original works by Muslim scholars who are thoroughly acquainted with the legacy, have a command over the modern sciences, and are prominent in creative ability and intellectual independence. All of these characteristics will qualify them to make original contributions to the Islamization of knowledge.

The purpose of this contribution will primarily be to expand the field of Islamization of knowledge and to lay down firm foundations for it by elucidating basic Islamic views, by presenting the issues of modern disciplines and their basic methodology, and by explaining the Islamic position concerning different disciplines and the way Islam considers the scientific issues in the light of Islamic principles. Samples of applied studies in these disciplines will be published to make the work of Muslim scholars in these disciplines more enlightened. This will help to bring home the message and purpose of the Islamization of knowledge and to determine how scholars may best contribute to realizing it through emulating and implementing it in their special fields of study, thereby setting an example and leading the way for the next generation.

Basic academic activities in the form of articles, discussions, and books will follow from the accomplished work and will be completed through implementing the Institute's agenda. This agenda includes cooperating with other scholars, hosting conferences and seminars, preparing periodicals, granting full-time or part-time fellowships for research and study on the premises of the Institute under its supervision. The supervision will depend upon the individual circumstances of each scholar and the financial resources of the Institute to support those among them who are not in a position to do so on their own. By accumulating these research works, by reawakening scholars and the educated, and by their readiness to acquire the qualifications necessary for the Islamization of knowledge, the Institute hopes to produce academic works on methodology for various disciplines that present and explain the genuine sublime Islamic view.

The ultimate goal of the Institute is to crystallize the scientific methodological works that are helpful in promoting Islamic knowledge and are useful as the first samples of academic works on Islamic methodology. This will encourage Muslim scholars, thinkers, and educated Muslims in general, to emulate and to identify themselves with the task of the Islamization of knowledge in respective fields of academic activity and intellectual work.

6. Priorities of Scientific Research

The priorities of the Institute in researching, transcribing, and compiling these works during the following five years will be as outlined below.

a. Methodology: As the basis for every scientific activity, the methodology of science must be thoroughly examined, improved, and developed to restore the comprehensive character of Islam and to regain contact with the genuine sources of Islamic thought with roots in revelation and reason. This developed methodology will be utilized to solve the problems of life and to meet its diverse intellectual, educational, and organizational requirements.

b. Behavioural Sciences: The primary importance of the sciences of psychology, sociology, and anthropology, along with the scientific methodology, lay in the fact that these sciences provide the theoretical bases upon which all the other social and human sciences rest. It is these very sciences and their hypotheses that, in the case of Western civilization, determine the definition of man, his ideals, his purposes in life, and his final goal. As such, these sciences symbolize the very essence of every other social science. All other social and human sciences are but practical applications of their hypotheses, views, and notions.

That is why the Islamization of these sciences and the elucidation of the Islamic view concerning them and their main issues occupy primary importance in the scheme of the Islamization of Knowledge. Writing textbooks in these sciences is a prerequisite for our ability to prepare methodological works in other disciplines. Indeed, without this step we would be missing an important link in the process of the Islamization of other social sciences and humanities, without which our aim cannot be realized.

c. Education and Political Science: The importance of these two sciences rests upon the fact that they represent the two basic links in formulating the being of the Ummah. The task of the former is to instruct the individual, while the latter determines the form and manner of the social system. Both of them are important and are closely related to the behavioural sciences, for they represent direct and practical application of their hypotheses and views. At present, the two disciplines underline two weak and palpably deficient aspects of the Ummah. The manner in which the individual in the Ummah is shaped, as well as the general organization of the society in Islamic countries, represent a standing contradiction of all that Islam stands for, of all that to which sincere Muslims aspire. They symbolize the weak Ummatic base, all the corruption, and the upheaval that plague the Ummah. It is, therefore, essential to move quickly and to reform these sciences by spelling out Islamic views regarding them, by studying them in depth, by taking a critical look at their hypotheses and resources, and by introducing the corresponding Islamic alternatives and hypotheses, which are based upon clear, well-substantiated argument and which offer a viable base for further construction and expansion.

d. Economics, Administration, Communications, and the Arts: Generally speaking, these sciences and arts provide us with important means for the smooth flow of human life. They seek to direct the course of social activity. They underlie the various fields that we have mentioned and help in forming the basic structure of Muslim society. As these disciplines also are closely related to the hypotheses of the behavioural sciences, work in them is easier and relatively less effort should be needed to Islamize them.

The Institute has already started work on the Islamization of the aforementioned ten sciences, along with the elucidation of basic Islamic views concerning them, by convening international conferences and organizing academic study circles. These events are attended by Muslim scholars from all parts of the world. That is why the Institute has embarked upon the preparation of authorized works. For the same reason, the Institute publishes books, monographs, research papers, and journals that deal with various issues and disciplines and works on making them available to the educated and the learned scholars. The agenda of the Institute in this regard is fairly broad, multifarious, and full of rich promise by the help and bounty from Allah (SWT). There is increasing realization among scholars and the educated classes of the importance of the Islamization of knowledge in formulating any firm and stable Islamic ideological basis, which allows for scholarly cooperation with the Institute to accomplish the goals of the agenda.

7. Preparation of Academic Cadres

Obviously, the issues of the crisis of Islamic thought, the question of the Islamization of knowledge, the duality of the educational system, and the need for Islamizing and unifying this system have all, to this day, largely remained in the realm of academic speculation. Likewise, it is obvious that the number of intellectuals and educated people, learned in both Islamic and contemporary disciplines and endowed with creativity and ability to present ideas in the fields of Islamic thought and the Islamization of knowledge, is very limited indeed. The number of those willing to come forward, or whose day-to-day, ordinary preoccupations in life allow them to undertake any such assiduous intellectual and educational work in these fields, is even smaller. As such, the Institute has no choice but to exert all its efforts and to use all its resources in order to prepare the required academic cadres and to help them perform their role in the Islamization of knowledge and to transmit their experience to younger students.

The underlying reason for the Institute's eagerness to prepare academic cadres is its desire to make amends for past disappointment, confusion, and negligence that arose not from any flaw or weakness in Islamic thought but, rather, from the absence of the requisite cadres to carry out the necessary functions. These past disappointments were sometimes caused by our failure to prepare and equip these cadres adequately with the requisite attributes as the bearers of Islamic ideology, which would give them the ability to apply it to practical life. In our view, this has been the most important reason for the failure of many academic and educational organizations that, in one way or another, sought to advance the cause of the Islamization of knowledge-a cause to which the Association of Muslim Social Scientists is dedicated. They failed because they did not fully realize the importance of training the future academic cadres on right and sound lines.

As such, the activities of the Institute are not confined to crystallizing thought, spreading the message, holding discussions, and publishing books. Its activities include preparing such cadres as are well-trained and adequately equipped to bear the Divine message and to lead the way by their pioneering work. As envisaged by the agenda of the Institute, the preparation of the requisite cadres will be accomplished in a number of ways and on various levels, such as through academic and educational fellowships, professorial studies, postdoctoral studies, university and higher studies, stipends for study, and supervision of the university theses. These are explained below in detail.

a. Scholarships: Academic fellowships are important means of preparing academic cadres and developing their faculties pertaining to any particular field of study or research. Normally, all scholars and learned teachers look for academic centres with a suitable academic atmosphere and an ability to provide library facilities to pursue their intellectual work, either during their summer vacations or during the school year. In these centres, academic research is carried out and intellectual dialogues take place that leave a deep imprint on the subsequent research and studies of these scholars.

Naturally, the Institute is a unique academic centre for Muslim scholars to pursue their research and work. The presence at the Institute of a team of some of the most eminent scholars, whose original work is of outstanding merit in the field of the Islamization of knowledge, all the more enhances the importance of the Institute in this respect.

As for those Muslim scholars who would like to pursue academic work in a field relevant to the Islamization of knowledge at their own expense or at the expense of their universities or academic organizations, the Institute can offer them the necessary technical services, library facilities, and opportunities for intellectual dialog in their specific academic topics that are related to Islamic ideology and the Islamization of knowledge.

As to cases in which pursuit of academic activity involves financial commitment to support the scholar, these will depend upon a number of factors, including the availability of financial resources, the importance of the project that a scholar might propose to pursue, the policy of the Institute concerning the project, and the extent to which a scholar is really qualified to pursue such a project or to contribute to a particular field.

The Institute looks hopefully to the prosperous members of the Muslim community and to Islamic institutions interested in the Islamization of knowledge and the reformation of Islamic thought for donations and study grants so that adequate provision can be made for the financial support of researchers in various fields.

b. Training Grants: This type of study is meant for doctoral degree.

holders whose training in their specializations has reached the highest level but who look forward to adding to their share of Islamic knowledge and to the academic concepts of the Islamization of knowledge under the supervision of scholars in the Institute.

A special program is prepared for this type of training grant recipient in which staff members of the Institute will chair seminars, reading sessions, symposiums, and discussions that will enhance their preparation in various aspects of knowledge required for a mastery of the sources of Islamic Thought, Islamic issues, and the concepts of the Islamization of knowledge. During the program and under the supervision of a faculty member, each recipient will prepare a paper on one of the issues of the Islamization of knowledge for publication as a pioneer work in this area.

Such in-service training programs are among the shortest and most fruitful programs in training high-calibre specialists. But the number of recipients to be given a chance to follow such a program of study is limited by the number of training grants available and the amount of living costs the Institute can afford.

c. Graduate Studies: This is the most widely known way of training academic cadres. It involves selecting outstanding graduates in social sciences and the humanities and registering them in graduate programs that will further train them in their specialization. The Institute will introduce an Islamic program that will familiarize those graduates with the sources of Islamic thought and the necessary tools to utilize those sources. This special program will help them comprehend the Islamic legacy and its contributions; it will initiate them into the various aspects and methods of the Islamization of knowledge; it will also help them gear their theses toward the issues of reforming Islamic thought and its methodology as well as the Islamization of knowledge. All this is to be done within their respective specializations and under the meticulous supervision of the Institute's faculty. This will implement the preparation of academic cadres of Islamic youth of the highest calibre in their specializations, characterized by capability, academic excellence, and Islamic knowledge. Their theses will contribute to the work toward the Islamization of knowledge, including the crystallization of its concepts and its scientific application in contemporary conditions.

The Institute is technically capable of arranging such programs and keenly desires to accomplish the task not only because of interest in the Islamization of knowledge but, also, due to the increasing difficulties and pressures on the Muslim youth to adopt concepts that are adverse to their Ummah, with roots in historical designs against the Ummah, the effects of which can no longer escape observation, pressures that inspire issues, and precepts that hamper their Islamic scholarly development and harm the civilizational edifice of the Ummah.

The Institute has already incorporated an Institute for Higher Studies, which will in the near future establish an alternative program in the area of social sciences and the humanities.

d. Undergraduate Studies: One essential requisite of good training of youth in general, students, and academic cadres of a nation is to imbue them with the principles, values, and philosophy of life that can penetrate their inner self and become part of their personality. The earlier the preparation of youth, the deeper the effect and the lighter the effort.

Planning the undergraduate level, the Islamic way, which builds up knowledge and methodology with Islamic goals and values in view, should be the first goal. No Ummah will rise unless its generations are provided with the right education at the undergraduate level that imbues them with its beliefs, aims, thoughts, way of life, and interests.

However, undergraduate programs in various fields of knowledge planned along Islamic concepts and methodology do not exist today, because recasting knowledge on a genuine Islamic basis is still in its infancy and the academic cadres to implement such a task have not yet been prepared.

It is hoped that, in the foreseeable future, the Institute, together with the universities of the Muslim world, will contribute more to the efforts exerted in this area. At present, the Institute will limit its share to joint work geared toward laying the foundations of Islamic knowledge and toward writing textbooks in various disciplines. This will make the task easier for universities and other academic institutions with enough financial resources to provide for Islamic programs that are suitable for the present stage.

e. University Textbooks and Their Importance: Although staffing in thc undergraduate classes is not among the prime purposes of the Institute at present, serving the undergraduate level is central to its interest. Such service, rendered by the Institute, comes as the fruit of intensive and varied efforts exerted in the areas of mastering of Islamic legacy and contemporary knowledge, in writing books, providing grants, hosting symposiums, preparing publications, providing tuition programs, and providing university textbooks. These all have the specific aims of crystallizing Islamic thought and methodology and making Islamic knowledge an actual fact.

University textbooks are important for reforming Islamic thought and for the Islamization of knowledge because they are essential for bringing to fruition an important stage of forming the Muslim mentality and its academic and technical skills. Additionally, these books are essential tools in presenting complementary scientific models that are indispensable for laying firm foundations for Islamizing knowledge.

The university textbook is detailed. It is both comprehensive and critical, as well as systematically representative of its line of specialization. Thus, university textbooks, in a broad sense, represent a comprehensive image of contemporary academia and thought, which is, in turn, the image of the civilization of the Ummah. Thus, the Institute, by concentrating upon the university textbook, will assert its interest in the vital undergraduate stage of university education.

f. Academic Grants and Supervision: An important aspect in the future of the Ummah and its smooth civilizational progress of which we must take note is the manner in which, at present, the way of thinking of the educated elements of the Ummah and of its ideological, political, and social leadership is being moulded in the set Western pattern that prevails in Western countries. It was because the West politically dominated the Islamic world that it found itself constrained to imitate and copy others. Added to this was the awareness of cultural backwardness, the desire to face new challenges, and the desire to counter the onslaughts of the greedy powers these and some other factors caused hosts of young men and educated people to leave their homelands. They went to some of the European metropolises, among which London and Paris stand out prominently as they are the capital cities of the traditional colonial powers that held sway over the Islamic lands from the Pacific Ocean and the China Sea to the Atlantic Ocean.

Since the emergence of the United States and the Soviet Union as the two dominant powers in the world, the methods of subjugation and manipulation have changed. Now political dominance goes hand-in-hand with the emphasis upon ideological, cultural, and economic domination and the use of political means to achieve the objectives of the dominant powers in the course of their international rivalries. Thousands of educated people and young men and women from the Islamic world, outside the Soviet bloc, have steadily been shifted to the United States and its universities, so that Western style intellectual and political leadership may be created among them to safeguard Western interests, objectives, and designs.

The Institute realizes that, in view of their importance, it must attend to the needs of these vast numbers of educated people and offer them help to make their stay at various universities and organizations in the United States really worthwhile and beneficial. This is being offered through a project of academic awards by which we can help these scholars in the higher stages of the masters and doctoral programs. We seek to cater to their welfare in two ways.

First, we must enlist the cooperation of Muslim scholars working in Western universities and elsewhere to supervise these youths, to guide them in their academic activities, and to lend them all possible help to complete their essential Islamic knowledge and to adopt a right and independent approach to their studies. Help from Muslim scholars also is needed to inspire these topics that tackle issues which really concern the Ummah and are helpful in elucidating its vision. This will help to make their theses a means of creative participation for these promising scholars in the service of humanity, and of suggesting academic alternatives inspired by Islamic vision for solving the problems confronting the world. These theses should be a means of tackling the issue of the Islamization of knowledge instead of allowing these theses and studies to be used as a means of moulding the Muslim mind into a completely alien Western pattern. Such theses should not be used for exploiting Muslim intellect to further the interests and objectives of alien powers nor as a means of collecting vital information to be manipulated by alien teachers and organizations.

Second, is offering material support to promising scholars of outstanding merit. Such support will be offered to young university-age Muslim students who are endowed with creative powers or those who have been chosen to pursue studies in fields that are important to the Ummatic goals and the objectives of the Institute. Its goals include ideological reformation, the Islamization of knowledge, and the presentation of genuine alternatives to and solutions for the difficulties and major problems of the Ummah. This material support will offer fields of study that are essential to providing special skills required by a Muslim country or a community of Muslim emigrants where the absence of such skills may cause serious setbacks and problems.

Chapter VI: Indispensable clarifications

At the end of this treatise on the Institute's vision regarding the malaise of the Ummah, the most urgent Islamic priorities, and the work and organization required to deal with them, we would like to briefly explain some of the pressing issues concerning this vision. This explanation is necessary in order to coordinate the efforts of various sincere persons- scholars, thinkers, and the educated among the Ummah - toward realizing the following objectives:

A. General Islamization

Anyone familiar with the condition of the Ummah at the present time knows that, without an integrated overall vision, its present crisis cannot be resolved successfully and that concentrating upon any particular aspect or important issue at the cost of others (whatever the justification or reasons for so doing) is not enough. We must move with intelligence and fortitude to overcome the obstacles and forces-material or intellectual, that have so far prevented us from equipping ourselves properly to prepare individuals and society to provide a base for the Islamic civilizational pattern.

Of the diverse alien slogans raised in the long history of the Ummah, there are two-one of "westernization" and the other of "modernization"-that are prominent. It is high time that we march ahead and unfurl the banner of "Islamization". This goal is ingrained in the very conscience of the Ummah and emanates from the very depths of its being. It must, therefore, be right to regard "Islamization" as the goal of the Ummah and of all its constituents, guiding its onward march as its brilliant star. In the end, slogans such as "westernization" and "modernization" are redundant and superfluous and will become obsolete. The Ummah is Islamic in creed, psychology, ideals, and history and the goal of "Islamization" embraces both the "contemporary" and the "modern". The only difference is that "Islamization" also acts as a guiding principle that directs human effort and leaves little room for misguidance and deception.

Thus, anyone who understands the true significance of Islam as a guide and as a magnanimous and comprehensive program of reformation knows that "Islamization" is, of necessity, contemporary and modern. Those who do understand will eagerly seek and clamour for its knowledge. The only Director of the process of Islamization is Allah (SWT), and its manual of operation is Islam itself - Islamic ideals and Islamic norms.

It must be made explicit here that, in fact, "Islamization" represents the truth, the justice, the transformation, and the reformation that concerns all Muslims. Its care and concern, by definition, extends to all human beings. It seeks to bestow dignity and honour upon all humans living on this earth. "Islamization" is the call that a divinely based civilization has addressed to the present world, which is torn apart with disaster looming large and clear. A true Muslim is the standard bearer of that mission, and he/she represents all salutary norms and values, symbolizing in practice the comprehensive model of a civilization based upon truth, justice, peace, and security. Islamic civilization is the best one suited for the current age. It is the boon that all the wise and learned, and those imbued with insight and living conscience, have been awaiting all these centuries.

B. Islamization of Knowledge

It must be made clear that the "Islamization of knowledge" represents only one aspect of "Islamization". In its entirety, "Islamization of knowledge" is the comprehensive, normative framework for individuals and society, for thought and action, for education and practice, for knowledge and organization, for the rulers and the ruled, for this world and for the world to come. By applying "Islamization" to everything one does, a Muslim seeks the pleasure of Allah (SWT) by practicing what is true and just, through transformation and improvement, to achieve happiness, peace and security in this life as well as in the hereafter.

The "Islamization of knowledge" is of fundamental importance and occupies foremost priority in actualizing "Islamization". It is concerned with thought, ideology, and a normative and ideational human pattern-and how such a pattern, its constituents, its roots in reason, psyche, and conscience may be built. This makes the "Islamization of knowledge" a prerequisite as a foundation for erecting the superstructure of the Ummah, for forming its individual and collective outlook on life, and for developing both its ideological and practical aspects. Therefore, the "Islamization of knowledge" cannot be neglected, nor can its priority be overlooked or buried beneath heavy pressures of political, economic, and military problems of the Ummah. At a time when we are forced to fight and defend ourselves on political, economic, and military fronts, these efforts may prove abortive and may simply dissipate the resources and energies of the Ummah unless we organize our struggle properly and develop the real powerbase of the Ummah. This can be accomplished by developing its ideological power and the power of the "Islamization of knowledge to effectively harness its full potential and energies. It is, therefore, necessary to build and restructure correct principles for genuine "Islamic intellection" and to create the conditions conducive to its existence and growth by erecting the lofty edifice of "Islamic knowledge".

"Islamic knowledge", or the "Islamization of knowledge", requires a proper and comprehensive Islamic methodology that seeks guidance from the revelation but does not render reason inert nor suspend its role. It reflects the objectives, norms, and ultimate purposes of revelation. It studies and grasps the guidance given by revelation to individuals and society for constructing, transforming, and improving all that Allah (SWT) has created. It teaches us how to formulate and to understand our mutuality and reciprocation and how to utilize them to our benefit. All this is necessary in order to understand this universe and its laws so that our work reflects its Divine Unity.

Through the "Islamization of knowledge", the Ummah is cognizant of the need for and importance of the scientific and cultural achievements that the human race has inherited and achieved. However, these must be thoroughly examined and critically checked in the light of Islam, its comprehensive norms, its guidance, and its ideals.

The "Islamization of knowledge" represents a type of knowledge based upon revealed norms and ideals of the Divine message. It is related to all that is true, valuable, and precious in the legacy of the Ummah and the thought- content of its scholars and thinkers over the centuries.

The "Islamization of Knowledge" signifies not just "norms and ideals", nor does it mean "individual meditations", nor is it just "a history and a legacy". It is, rather, a way and a method to formulate a methodological, scientific, mental approach to the humanities, social sciences, and applied sciences.

The "Islamization of knowledge" is scientific knowledg - the knowledge that originates from Divine norms and ideals. It is rational in its outlook, its approach, its search, its critical examination of the problems of life, and its treatment of individual society, nature, and the laws that govern its workings.

For the Ummah, the "Islamization of Knowledge" is, at the moment, a matter of utmost priority. It aims at developing a methodology for Islamic ideology-purifying it of all the aberration, corruption, isolation, inertia, and division from which it has suffered over the centuries. It aims at reinvigorating Islamic thought and its methodology by giving it access to the main fountainheads of the legacy of the Ummah. Likewise, its purpose is to achieve mastery of Islamic thought in various branches of human knowledge (social, physical or practically applied) in order to build a sound contemporary Islamic base for dynamic action in all spheres of life and civilization.

The prime importance of the "Islamization of knowledge", the reformation of thought and methodology of the legacy and contemporary sciences, does not imply suspension of all other activities. Rather, it means that we should give due attention to the provision of various spiritual and material resources for reformation in the intellectual sphere. This is important in order to coordinate and properly utilize various reformatory efforts, human sacrifices, and material expenditures. In the absence of such reformation of thought and methodology, all of these are bound to be ineffective and insipid.

The proposed "Islamization of knowledge" will harness the intellect and the ideology and will provide a sound methodology for the dire needs of the Ummah. This, in turn, will enable it to confront contemporary challenges and to furnish it with a powerbase, a rationale, a vision, and an ideologically oriented civilizational methodology that will build a superstructure for improvement and welfare. The Ummah lacks not in sincerity, nor in norms, nor in human and material potential. It does, however, lack sound thought, a meticulous methodology, and a clear vision to guide its steps and to give it an ideal for which it should strive and in the light of which its new generations should be reared.

It is important to remember that, without reformation of thought and methodology and in the absence of a genuine and clear vision, all efforts are bound to be ineffective and all sacrifices to be useless. This is how the civilization of Islam and those before it grew and progressed. The history of Europe's confrontation with Islam shows how, in the face of the assault by 'Uthmani Muslims, it found itself weak and suffered defeats that spurred it into action. This difficult period of confrontation was transformed when Europe reformed its thought through imitating the achievements of Muslim culture as reflected in its norms, ideals, and legacy. This is a part of history that is well known to us, and its consequences are all too obvious.

It does not become the Muslim to ignore or refuse to learn from the past experiences of others. The time for sermonizing is gone. We must now set our priorities right and refuse to neglect the basic issues. No matter how strong the pull of events or how fierce the attacks upon us, they should not prevent us from rebuilding our real strength-a kind of strength that alone can generate the proper efforts in correct measure and in the proper direction. For the sake of clear vision and smooth progress toward eliminating any misunderstanding from the minds of wise and sincere people, we would like to emphasize that giving priority to the "Islamization of knowledge" does not imply any contradiction or negation of Ummatic efforts in other fields of life. Rather, it seeks to complement these efforts, sharing with them a common burden and forging a relationship with them in such a way that they strengthen and support each other-each supplying the requirements of the other.

The objectives of the "Islamization of knowledge" are to perfect the tools necessary for the Ummah to progress smoothly in its Islamic role, to furnish it with the essential powers and faculties for its proper functioning, and to clarify its vision and its methodology. Achieving these objectives will better prepare the Ummah to succeed in its struggle with a changeable contemporary life that offers vast opportunities as well as serious challenges.

In its widest sense, "Islamization" means a framework for human life, civilization, and human transformation. It determines the purpose of every activity, struggle, action, and Islamic social organization. It gives human life purpose and charts its course. But it would be wrong to neglect or underrate the importance of any of the other diverse aspects of life. Rather, each aspect should receive due attention and consideration. Any task that the Ummah undertakes should be supported by whatever efforts may be necessary to resolve a problem at a particular point in time or a specific stage. Giving priority to the "Islamization of knowledge" does not cancel other priorities nor does it belittle the significance of political, economic, social, academic, and military efforts. It simply means that the "Islamization of knowledge" is urgent, a prerequisite, a necessary condition, that we are committed to fulfil as a preamble to other requirements in order to achieve perfection in provision, clarification of vision, revival of the power to build, and the ability to withstand encounters.

C. Priorities in the Ummatic Scheme for the "Islamization of Knowledge"

For the full realization of the "Islamization of knowledge" and in order to make it yield beneficial results, certain rules must be clearly laid down and certain aspects must be perfected and completed before we can say that the "Islamization of knowledge" has been fully realized; that it has, indeed, become an actual institution of the Muslim community; and that it is able to render help to the Ummah in resolving its problems by genuine thinking and creativity.

Before we can erect any edifice of the "Islamization of knowledge", we need to master the fundamental principles of Islam and Islamic legacy and gain the proper knowledge of contemporary social and applied sciences. We also must be fully acquainted with the Islamic vision and Islamic ideological and methodological notions prior to any stage of "contribution and creativity", during which various sciences and branches of Islamic lore and Islamic civilization will flourish in full splendour. This process of the "Islamization of knowledge" in the life of the Ummah will pass through two elementary stages, as explained below.

Stage One

a. Mastery of the Modern Sciences: Mastery of the modern sciences means that Muslim scholars of modern sciences must have command over those sciences. To understand their objectives and the history and circumstances of their development, they must fully understand their issues and methodology and be able to approach them in their totality. They also must know the critical, analytical, and objective aspects of those sciences in their Western perspective and in the light of the true Islamic viewpoint.

Through their mastery of modern sciences, Muslim scholars will have access to both the capabilities and knowledge that human civilization has so far accumulated. Additionally, it will provide those scholars with valuable information and a methodology with which to establish a firm Islamic theoretical basis for various aspects of social life. These aspects represent the important facets of human nature and the actual environmental conditions that are the subject of study, meditation, guidance, and instruction of those scholars. Such perfect mastery will also remove the scourge of limitation, mimicry, and masquerade from Islamic life and will open up new vistas of dynamic creativity.

b. Mastery of the Legacy: The purpose of gaining mastery over modern disciplines is to benefit from the common human heritage, to assimilate those disciplines, and to represent them in their proper perspective so that they should serve Islamic ideology, Islamic vision, and Islamic ideals in the present age. To achieve this purpose, the Muslim scholar must, of necessity, have command over the fundamentals of Islam as embodied in the Qur'an and the Sunnah. He must have an adequate understanding of the various Islamic texts that relate to his special field. He also must be fully conversant with the Islamic legacy - sifting what is correct, useful, precious, and has emanated from genuine Islamic spirit and ideals from what is spurious and has been overplayed with diverse aberrations, barren sophistic discussions, or deviations and maladies that have afflicted the spiritual life of the Ummah and its thinking over the centuries. Such mastery may be gained by studying selections from the legacy relating to all branches of science, art, and life. Such selections can be prepared along with critical and analytical notes on the legacy and then made available to research scholars for a fuller understanding of the vision of the ancestors as reflected in their behaviour. These selections will explain how the vision moved the legacy, how it evolved a genuine and powerful methodology, and how the ancestors used it to resolve the problems and issues that faced them, thereby opening up new and broader horizons for transformation, development and civilization.

Stage Two

a. Defining the Main Issues: Before we can embark upon any rational and creative venture, we must first be able to clearly define the issues and challenges confronting us and determine which we want to resolve.

It is therefore incumbent upon the Muslim intellectual to define precisely in his particular field of study the nature of the problems that face the Ummah or the entire human race, problems the resolution of which should occupy the prime time and efforts for a Muslim thinker. Until such time as the Muslim intellect is free and capable of making any original contribution, it is important that Muslim intellectuals begin to define the problems facing the Ummah and to decide upon their priorities so that the Islamic vision may yield its beneficial fruits. In this connection, it is important for Muslim intellectuals to realize that the economic, social, and political problems of the Ummah - very serious problems by any standard-are, in fact, just side effects of the real malaise of the

Ummah. It is the cloudiness of vision, the weakness and deterioration of contemporary Islamic thought and its methodology, that underlies such present maladies as corruption, inefficient performance, inadequate education, and weakness of the moral character of the Ummah.

It is likewise the duty of Muslim intellectuals to define the problems and challenges facing the human race today, for it is Muslims alone who, despite their cultural backwardness, possess the remedy-Islam. If they explain it properly to other people and convey its true message to them, Muslims may provide non-Muslims with a key for solving their difficult problems; Islam alone can provide man with a firm base for his simultaneous religious and moral growth along with material progress and prosperity. It is Islam that can rebuild the entire human life in accordance with the will of its Creator, who ordained man to be His vicegerent on earth and charged him to believe in truth and to strive for improvement and transformation.

Equipped with Islamic vision, Muslim intellectuals can tackle the problems confronting the human race today. The Ummah, which is blessed with the Islamic vision, does, in fact, represent truth. It can bring hope and salvation to suffering humanity, whose cause is forgotten and lost amid rivalries of the imperialists and the revolutionaries from whose clutch's humanity struggles in vain to free itself, Racial prejudices are rampant and have dealt a death blow to the bonds of mutual love and care that should bind humans together.

Whatever good is left is also in jeopardy and is drowned in drinking or lost in narcotics. There is chaos in sexual relations and a breakdown in family life. Ignorance and apathy, tyrannical governments, accumulation of arms, aggression against nature that threatens to upset the entire ecological balance on earth-all these and other evils are spreading like wildfire, and there is no power except Islam to counter or curb them. Thanks to its sound ideology, Islam alone can envisage and implement plans to check these evils. By fulfilling its trust and mission, the Ummah can achieve felicity for itself as well as for the entire human race. Showing humanity, the way to happiness and prosperity within an overall framework of justice, honour, and consideration for humanity constitutes the essence of the Ummah's vision and mission. It underpins all planning for the present age to enable the Ummah to live up to its challenges.

b. Islamic Creativity and Initiative: "Islamic creativity", "Islamic contribution", and the full realization of "Islamization" in the being of the Ummah and its civilizational direction will follow the command and mastery of the fundamentals of Islam and Islamic legacy along with a thorough acquaintance with modern sciences. The legacy, in conjunction with Islamic creativity, will use analytical, critical methodologies to integrate the Islamic vision and outlook with the facts of contemporary life. In the interests of improvement and transformation, the Islamic vision should focus upon and resolve the problems and difficulties of contemporary life. Thus, prepared and equipped, Islamic ideology will resume its initiative by making positive contributions, by suggesting alternatives to cure present evils, by countering the threats faced by the Ummah, and by assuming the lead in fields of intellectual and cultural reformation to all people on earth, thereby liberating them, transforming them, and directing their steps on to the right path. It is the duty of the creative Muslim intellect, and of the genuine Muslim thinker to quicken this pace on the road of inquiry and self-preparation; to rectify the damage suffered by the Islamic civilization during the long period of its backwardness; and to excel in the sciences, knowledge, civilization, and transformation, thereby opening far wider horizons than ever before reached by humanity and modern science.

The Muslim intellect must develop alternative solutions and proper standards as defined in Islam through its Shari'ah, morals, education, objectives, and ideals. To realize this, the Muslim must acquire the requisite means and become proficient in using manipulating tools, otherwise Islamic thought may become introverted and haphazard; it may lack the vigour to tackle problems or to face new challenges; and it may become out of touch with day-to-day life.

When the Ummah is thus prepared to contribute afresh intellectually, its contribution will no longer be confined to the isolated anthologies of university textbooks or be limited to specific cadres and programs of studies. Instead, it will pervade its entire being with incessant outbursts of creative genius on all sides, emanating from its deeply embedded Ummatic consciousness and covering all fields of life. That will represent the march of the Ummah with all its energies for contributing to the marvellous achievement of certain geniuses, the like of whom the Ummah cannot breed for centuries.

D. Priorities of the Institute's Plan

The previous section was titled: Priorities in the Ummatic Scheme for the 'Islamization of knowledge. As it mentioned, the process of the "Islamization of knowledge" on the Ummatic level ideally must progress through two stages, each with four different aspects. These two stages are "the stage of mastery and perfect workmanship" and "the stage of independence and creative contribution".

The stage of "mastery and perfect workmanship" will include two things: command of the Islamic legacy and mastery over the contemporary sciences. The "stage of creativity and independence" will follow once the acme in vision and methodology is realized. This second stage will provide us with clear, useful, and beneficial knowledge, serenity of performance and a base for raising a strong, firm civilizational edifice.

What is true about other nations respecting these stages is equally applicable to individuals and academic cadres and to the process of formulating the academic methodology or the basic principles of the Islamization of knowledge. Individuals and the Ummah as a whole must have mastery over the Islamic legacy and command over modern sciences before either the individual or the Ummah is in a position to benefit from its creative potential.

The Institute hopes to integrate the efforts of various academic organizations and individual members of the Ummah to pave the way for gaining mastery and command over the fundamentals and the previous treasures of the legacy. This can be achieved by classifying them and making them accessible to scholars in addition to offering all possible help necessary for assimilating and mastering the legacy. Similar help may be offered to those striving to gain mastery over modern sciences. For them, model studies may be organized. Comprehensive and critical anthologies may be prepared from such works as are prominent for their excellent workmanship and erudition. These anthologies will cover both literal aspects and details and may be helpful in understanding general principles and their origins, thereby making their study useful for creating independent outlook and insight.

The efforts for gaining mastery over the modern sciences must not be confined to a limited group of scholars living abroad in foreign lands who possess limited proficiency in foreign languages. Rather, it should involve the entire academic and educated cadres of the Ummah. This can be achieved by translating all important works into Arabic and other languages to provide the educated with the latest information in the most suitable form. All that we need is to establish a few schools of translation and some companies to print, distribute, and circulate such translations when they are ready. For this purpose, private initiative and commercial service also may be encouraged to achieve all the conditions for the requisite mastery and to prepare for creative contribution and performance on the Ummatic level and not on the restricted level. Previously, creative contributions were on the restricted level, through isolated chance contributions of certain extraordinary men of genius, who are no longer to be found anywhere except in the pages of history, commemorative services, special celebrations, or citations of honour where they are mentioned only to console and exalt.

For this preparation, the work plan of the Institute does not, strictly speaking, envision binding adherence to this order or these stages in its future course.

Since its inception, the Institute has been actively engaged in formulating rules regarding basic principles, notions, and methodology of the Islamic vision. At the same time, it also has been calling for "Islamization" and "Islamization of knowledge", stressing the need for action to achieve mastery and command both in the field of the legacy and modern sciences, and making provisions for acquiring the requisite skills and resources for it.

Through authorizing the writing of "new original material," the Institute hopes to facilitate the task of formulating the basic rules and principles of the methodology of the Islamic vision. This involves awarding fellowships to individual scholars of outstanding merit who are endowed with originality and, at the same time, are well-versed in the legacy as well as in the modern sciences and with recording the results of their research. These exploratory writings may serve as a beacon to elucidate further the principles of the "Islamization of knowledge", to generate independence of thought and induce creativity, and to enable us to exploit them effectively.

But the Institute is working both to formulate the theoretical bases and principles of the Islamic vision and its methodology and also is engaged in preparing basic studies to complement the efforts directed at gaining mastery and command of the disciplines. Such effort involves preparing studies of high quality that cover the fundamental principles of Islam and the Islamic legacy, as well as conducting a comprehensive critical survey of modern disciplines. Such studies will serve as a model for the educated members of the Ummah to follow in their inquiries and work, which must be properly presented as an integral part of the education of the Ummah and the result of the labours of its own scholars and educated members.

The Institute is fully aware that it cannot accomplish all this alone, nor is this expected of it. It is a tremendous task that involves a thorough investigation into various disciplines and, as such, can only be accomplished by the Ummah as a whole. All its organizations must participate, and anyone with the requisite academic and intellectual qualifications should contribute. The Institute only seeks to prepare the minds and smooth the way by making available models in palpable form. The Institute also seeks to help the Ummah in its efforts toward reconstructing its intellection, which is necessary for it to succeed with any of its individual or collective endeavours. Without this reconstruction, no amount of faith, sincerity, sacrifice, and striving can really bear fruit.

To realize this objective, the Institute convenes meetings, arranges discussions, and produces publications. It seeks to educate, coordinate, and cooperate with all those who may be interested in the Institute's work and programs and who are willing to assist it in the discharge of its duty. The Institute calls upon all individuals and organizations, private and public, for their help and support. They are invited to visit or write the Institute, to know and become convinced in order that, together, we can forge ahead - joining and coordinating efforts to make the truth and word of Allah (SWT) prevail.

This is the message of the Institute and its sole objective. The Institute and its members and sisters are quite confident of Divine help. They look forward to their brothers and sisters' response to their call to come forward with sincere efforts to realize the goal, surmounting the multifarious obstacles. that might stand in the way, Allah (SWT) willing.

We seek help, guidance, strength, and rectitude from Allah (SWT), Who hears and responds to the prayers of His servants. And let our prayer close with the words: "Praise be to Allah (SWT), the Cherisher and Sustainer of all the worlds!"

Chapter VII: Financial requirements

Endowment and Investment

Restricting support for charitable work and public service to governments and official contributions, subject to numerous political, administrative, and routine limitations deprives the Ummah of one of the most important sources of support for enterprise and creative activity. This source is to be found in private charitable initiative and the good will of individuals and their zeal for general welfare and reformation.

The organizations rendering general charitable services are among the most important forms of social organization in the life of developed and stable societies. In such societies, charitable undertakings are eagerly protected and encouraged.

We witnessed the same phenomenon during the flourishing periods of the Ummah. Through generous self-perpetuating endowments, individuals expressed their charitable initiative and supported charitable private organizations. Thus, the institution of endowment (*waqf*) occupied a sacrosanct position in Islam; and it was not permissible for anyone to misuse the waqf or to divert its funds from their lofty purposes. Muslim individuals, organizations, and governments used to always try to support and strengthen endowments. They were protected as the main source of constant income to support certain charitable organizations. All the expenses of such organizations that were incurred in the course of their charitable services were met by the proceeds of these endowments. Thus, for centuries, these organizations in different parts of the Muslim world were able to serve the cause of education, public health, orphanages, shelters for the homeless, mosques and other vital institutions.

With the decline of the Ummah, the ideal of private charitable enterprise and charitable endowment suffered a setback and gradually vanished. The ways in which they fell prey to individual or collective greed and aggression were diverse. When imperialism had hegemony over the Islamic world, floodgates of Western ideas and philosophies that were hostile and inimical to the norms and legacy of the Ummah were thrown open, and Islamic charitable organizations were violently and most viciously attacked. They were deprived of their endowments and plundered and robbed under different pretexts. Of these organizations, only a few have managed to survive in most of the Muslim countries.

Today, the Ummah is deprived of this important economic sector. The unique spirit of sincere individual charity is gradually being whittled away. The Ummah's civilizational base and the edifice that rests upon it is threatened. This is due to an ever-increasing hold upon it of intellectually bankrupt, autocratic bureaucracy of various governmental departments. It is, therefore, necessary to revive the outlook of the Ummah in the field of general services and to encourage private charity within the framework of endowments. This should be done in such a way that these self-perpetuating endowments are once again able to play their role as sources of strength, generosity, donation. and protection, thereby allowing Islamic charitable organizations to fulfil their obligations.

The Institute cannot detach itself from the serious difficulties experienced by many of these charitable organizations and Islamic services on account of the paucity of requisite funds to support and finance their projects and welfare programs. During the course of their long association with certain Islamic organizations and through participation in their formation, the members of the Institute invariably noticed that such organizations were perpetually beset by the problem of shortage of funds because they depended, year after year, upon donations alone.

In the world of today, donations are difficult to come by and, wherever they do exist, are extremely scarce and scattered, requiring a lot of struggles on the part of those concerned to gain access to them. This inevitably affects activities and performance, and much precious time is lost in long journeys to collect such donations. Moreover, such journeys normally cause the dispersal of efforts and the dissipation of already rare talents and faculties.

In this regard, the Institute has consistently followed a different strategy. It has tried to avoid such pitfalls and problems by benefiting from opportunities that are available in its own immediate milieu. It has utilized the support that U.S. laws and its system offer to private enterprise aimed at encouraging people to participate in public works of charity. In keeping with this strategy, the Institute, in agreement with most of its patrons, has tried to generate financial resources in the United States by investing donated funds and by using their returns in various projects of the Institute. The Institute appeals to all well-to-do Muslims living in America or abroad to contribute whatever they can while benefiting from tax exemption laws. Let them donate whatever amounts they may be able to give for Islamic charitable organizations, such as the Institute, mosques, schools, Islamic centres and other important Muslim organizations active in the United States, thereby taking advantage of the tax concession on all such contributions.

It is the duty of Muslim governments and of Muslim entrepreneurs of America to realize the importance of this issue and to reroute all their taxes, or whatever portion of then is possible, for the service of their religion, their fellow Muslims, and eminently deserving Muslim organizations, among which are this Institute. This would be far better than letting this wealth go to organizations inimical to Islam to be used in exploiting Muslims and in desecrating their most holy places, organizations, and institutions.

www.ingramcontent.com/pod-product-compliance
Ingram Content Group UK Ltd.
Pitfield, Milton Keynes, MK11 3LW, UK
UKHW021407190726
13845UKWH00028B/934

9 788119 946730